EVERYBODY WINS!

150 Non-Competitive Games for Kids

Cynthia MacGregor

Adams Media Corporation
AVON, MASSACHUSETTS

DEDICATION

For Yvonne, my mother and biggest fan,
with love and appreciation

ACKNOWLEDGMENTS

As usual, I couldn't have done it without Vic Bobb.
Thanks also to John Davidson and Sheryl Pease.

Published by
Adams Media Corporation
57 Littlefield Street, Avon, MA 02322. U.S.A.
adamsmedia.com

ISBN: 1-58062-063-9

Printed in the United States of America.

J I H G F E D C

Library of Congress Cataloging-in-Publication Data
MacGregor, Cynthia.
Everybody wins! : 150 non-competitive games for kids / by Cynthia MacGregor.
p   cm.
Includes index.
ISBN 1-58062-063-9
1. Games. I. Title.
GV1203.M318   1998
790.1—dc21   98-8592
CIP

ILLUSTRATIONS BY BARRY LITTMANN

This book is available at quantity discounts for bulk purchases.
For information, call 1-800-872-5627.

CONTENTS

INTRODUCTION............................ ix

QUIET GAMES AND ACTIVITIES
Insta-Messages............................ 2
A-Maze-Ing 3
Buzz/Fizz..................................... 4
Beep! 6
The Word of the Hour 7
Substitute Nouns.......................... 9
A Matter of Perception.............. 10
Rules of Life 12
Creative Alibis 13
The _____ Family
    Memory Book......................... 14
Cause and Effect 16
I Want to Sell You a Kangaroo
    17

Family/Friends
    Memory Challenge 18
Early Memories 20
The _____ Family
    Dictionary 21
Don't Make Me Laugh.............. 22
The Wild Blue Yonder 23
A Wish List for the World 25
Word-and-Name Chains 26
Far-Fetched Connections 28

Head 'n Tail Categories 29
Tell Me a Me-Story 31
Chocolate Cake 32
Tongue Twisters 34
Secret Code Language 35
Coded Capers 36
Dictionary Challenge 38
Spellcheck................................... 39
Dictionary Bluff.......................... 40
Dictionary Add-Ons 41
One-for-All Scrabble................. 42
Rebuses 43
The R&D Department 44
Tiny Shoe 45
Inventions................................... 46
Describing Pairs 48
Powers of Perception 49
Three-at-a-Time Stories 51
Very Short Stories 52
Mangled Proverbs..................... 54
Spoonerisms............................... 55
"I One It" 56
Fortunately 57
High Dice 58
Non-Competitive
    Double Solitaire 59
Mystery Guest 60
Famous Pairs 62
Odd Couples 63
Tell Me My Fortune 64
Which Letter Wins? 67
Captions Outrageous 68
Mixed Media Alphabet Book .. 69
Who Am I? 70
Telephone 72

Back 'n' Forth Books................. 73
Do You Speak Splabble? 74
Guess the Outcome.................... 75
Design a Castle 76
And on the Eighth Day 77
Top Ten Lists 78

BEANBAG GAMES
Bucket Beanbag 81
Bucket Beanbag—
  "NFL" Version 84
Beanbag Squares 86
Beanbag Toss 90

OTHER ACTIVE GAMES
Chairs Aplenty 92
Musical Pile-Up......................... 93
Jellyseek 94
Sheetball 96
Scrambled Nonrace 97
Partnership Bowling.................. 98
Blob Tag 99
Three Deep 100

Statues.. 101
Duck Duck Goose 103
Go in and out the Window 104
The Fox and
  the Colored Eggs 105
The Ogre in the Attic 106
Hoop-De-Doo 107
Volley Up 111
Walk 'n' Roll............................. 112
Rock Around the Block 114
Wet Walk................................... 116
Don't Wake Me—
  I'm Sleeping 117
Button, Button,
  Who's Got the Button? 118
The Winning Room................... 119
A Trip to Peoria 121
Ring My Chimes 122
Grass Drills................................ 123
Keep It Up 127

ADVENTURES IN THE ARTS
Open Mike Night 130
Put on a Show 131
Puppet Theater 132
Sing Me a Song from
  the Good Old Days 134
An Augmented Chorus 136
Band Together 137
Family Song 138
Parodies 139
Picture It—Literally 140
Designing Kids 141
Family Symbol.......................... 142
Identi-Sketch 143
Oprah's On................................ 145
Thank You, and Good Night.. 146

Sell This! 148
Silly Stories.............................. 149
Draw That Scene 151
Jamie's Got a Hippo
    on Her Head 153
Draw a Whatzit 154
Two Types of Chain Stories.... 155
Cliffhanger Stories 157
Collaborating on a "Book" 159
Current Events Book 161
Couplets 163
Rhyme Fun............................... 164
A Rhyme in Time 166
Tall Tales about Objects 168
"This Is Your
    Roving Reporter" 170
Rainbow Array 171

MISCELLANEOUS ACTIVITIES
The Settlement
    of Arzagon XII 174
A House to Play House—
    or Other Games—In 177
Step School 178
Welcome to the Club 179
Cooperative License
    Plate Games 181
"What You Got There?" 183
Fine or Super-Fine?.................. 185
What's Cookin'? 186
Bakable Fun Dough 187
Clipping Coupons . . .
    of a Sort 188
Chips Ahoy 189
Construction Chips.................. 191
Build a City 192
Whither the Weather?.............. 193

Observation Test 195
Bobbing for Apples.................. 196
Makeovers—on Paper 197
Tin-Can Telephone 199
Clothespin Drop 200
Hat Trick 201
Floating Rainbows 202
Drawbacks 203
Secret Messages......................... 204
Invisible Ink Messages 205
What's That? 206
I Can Help You Learn.............. 207
Practice! Practice! 209
The Race Is On.......................... 210
The Joke's on You 211
House of Cards 212
How Many *Real* Feet?.............. 213
"Four out of Five Kids
    Surveyed Said . . ." 214

INTRODUCTION

So you used to think that when you had a second child, it would give your first child someone to play with, and you'd get a little peace and quiet? Or you can remember a time when you thought that if you invited a friend over to play with your child, the two of them would keep each other busy, and calm and quiet would reign?

You know better now, don't you? Kids, even the best-behaved of kids, argue, squabble, and outright fight when they're together, whether they're siblings, playmates, or even best friends.

Why?

Listen to the arguments and you'll hear the answer for yourself. Of course there's a fair amount of "She won't share!" or "I was playing with it first." But even more, you'll hear cries of "He cheated!" "It was my turn!" "I won and she won't admit it!" "You were not at the fourth square. You were only back here, you cheater!" (Throughout this book the pronouns *he* and *she* are used alternately.)

What's it all about? Competition! Everyone wants to be a winner; nobody likes losing. Even you probably don't like losing, whether it's at Bingo, at cards, or at beating the woman with the cartful of groceries to the check-out line. But at your age you've learned to handle life's losses more gracefully (I hope!), and you don't get bent out of shape when your son beats you at Monopoly or your

spouse yells "Gin!" and discards the six of spades that you needed to win.

At three, five, seven, nine, or even eleven, your child isn't as practiced as you at accepting defeat as transitory. This comes with both practice and maturity. But some days you may feel that if your kids get much more practice at losing, you're going to be gray-haired before they get to high school.

So what's the solution for a little peace and quiet?

Non-competitive games and activities.

If the kids aren't trying to beat each other at a game, to each be the Winner, to each emerge triumphant, there's a lot less cause for strife. Oh, I don't promise you eternal peace and quiet if you introduce non-competitive play into the picture, but I think it's safe to promise there'll be a lot less hollering, fighting, accusing, and general discord.

Whether it's your own two (or more) kids or your only child and his/her friends, when they play non-competitively, there's a lot less reason to argue and fight. And they can still have lots of fun. The games and other activities in this book are non-competitive, so everybody wins! There are athletic activities, quiet activities, activities that involve heavy-duty thinking, and activities that involve little more than daydreaming—something we all know kids are good at. Some will improve a skill or make them think a new way about something; others are just for fun … and what's wrong with a little fun?!

So introduce these activities to your kids and get ready to enjoy some peace and quiet. Get out of your mediator role—did you ever feel as if motherhood was the ideal training for a position as a labor mediator?—and get ready to enjoy some well-deserved silence, punctuated, perhaps, by some giggles from the other room. And maybe even some loud out-and-out laughter. But no squabbling.

CHAPTER ONE

QUIET GAMES AND ACTIVITIES

INSTA-MESSAGES

Here's a goofy game that will make the kids think *and* laugh. It's good for any number of players.

The first player calls out any letter of the alphabet. The second player then calls out a letter. Play continues with each player contributing a letter till ten have been called. As the letters are called, each player writes them down. Ultimately, all the players have the same ten letters written on their papers.

Now each player tries to craft a telegram-style message, ten words in length, each beginning with one of the ten letters, in the order given. For instance, if the ten letters are O B P D C D F B P T, one player might come up with OUR BAND PRACTICES DAILY. CONTRIBUTE DRUMSTICKS FOR BETTER PERCUSSION TONES. The other players will no doubt go off in totally different directions with their usage of the same ten letters.

Each player writes down his "telegram." When all the players are finished, the messages are read aloud. Then the players can start all over with ten more letters, if they wish, creating new insta-messages.

Pointers:

MATERIALS NEEDED:
Paper and pen or pencil for each player

AGE OR SKILL LEVEL:
Able to write and spell

♦ Since it's harder to find appropriate words beginning with Q, U, X, Z, probably Y, and possibly even V and W, it's best not to use at least the first four of those and possibly all seven.

♦ Any number can play. Technically one person can even amuse herself playing this game solo, but it's more fun in pairs or groups.

♦ Punctuation of any sort can be inserted anywhere within the ten letters.

♦ As with telegrams, words not absolutely essential to clarity may be omitted, especially words like *a*, *an*, *the*, and even *I* or *you*.

—Telegram—
Bring Dog
Outside And
Run Wild Until
He's Very Tired

A-MAZE-ING

Kids love mazes.

When you have two (or more) kids playing together, each can create a maze, then pass it to another child to solve. So pass out plenty of paper (scrap paper will do fine if it's large enough) and get those pencils sharpened.

Everyone has his own approach to maze-building, but it's probably easiest if the kids draw the outer parameters of the maze first. Then they can locate the entrance and the exit, and finally they can draw the actual maze inside, the labyrinthian series of blind alleys, false trails, and twisted connections that will baffle all but the most intrepid maze-searchers who seek their way from start to end.

Even young children can make a simple maze. It may not seem like much of a maze to you, but to another child around the same age, it should be just right. At that age, too, simply drawing a maze is practice in motor skills. Solving it is practice in problem-solving, deduction, and reasoning. Older kids will get practice in all

MATERIALS NEEDED:
Paper, pen, pencil, and eraser

AGE OR SKILL LEVEL:
Five and up

the above, too, and can extend their skills in drawing a far more complicated maze.

They'll quickly learn how—and how not—to construct a maze. They'll be reminded that they need to leave openings in the walls so that blind alleys and dead-end routes can be included to mislead the unwary maze-traveler.

Since they're bound to goof many times along the way, or to draw in a blind alley and then realize *that* would be the ideal place for part of the right path, it's best if they do their initial maze-drawing in pencil, with an eraser handy. Later, when they're content with their mazes, sure that the mazes have one—and only one—way to get from Start to End and have plenty of false trails too, they can go back over the pencil lines in pen.

The pencils will be needed again when everyone trades mazes and tries to trace his way through a friend's or sibling's maze.

BUZZ/FIZZ

In the traditional versions of the games of Buzz, Fizz, and Fizz-Buzz, all of which are games for two or more players, with no limit to the number who can play, a player making a mistake is out of the game. The last player left is the winner. Along the way, as players goof, everyone has a tendency to laugh.

Why not laugh without eliminating players?

In the non-competitive version of the games, the players play, occasionally make mistakes, and everyone laughs…but the game is simply over when you get to 100, without anyone being out.

For those not familiar with Buzz, it's a game involving the number seven. Players count aloud, avoiding saying any number that has a seven in it (such as "seventeen") or is a multiple of seven. The first player starts by saying "One." The second player responds with "Two." The third player (or the first, again, in a two-player game) chimes in with "Three." And so it goes up through "Six." But instead of the next player saying "Seven," the player whose turn it is says "Buzz."

MATERIALS NEEDED:
None

AGE OR SKILL LEVEL:
Able to count above twenty

And every time after that that a number either *contains a seven* or is *a multiple of seven*, the player whose turn it is must say "Buzz" instead of saying the number. Thus the call after "Six" is "Buzz," the call after "Thirteen" is "Buzz" (14 is a multiple of 7), the call after "Sixteen" is "Buzz" (17 contains a 7), and players would "Buzz" again in lieu of 21, 27, 28, 35, 37, 42, 47, 49, and so on.

A good approach to a non-competitive version of the game is "Let's see if we can get to 100 without anyone messing up." Instead of competing, the players are united in a purpose … and will be united in laughter when someone goofs up and says "Seven" or "Twenty-one," or "Thirty-seven." It's virtually inevitable that someone will err. (It's also an error to "Buzz" on a wrong number—a number that does *not* contain a seven and is *not* a multiple of seven either.)

The game of Fizz is very similar. In fact, the only difference is that instead of "Buzz"ing on numbers containing a seven or that are multiples of seven, players call "Fizz" on numbers that contain a five or are multiples of five. Thus: "One," "Two," "Three," "Four," "Fizz," "Six," "Seven," "Eight," "Nine," "Fizz," and so on. Players would call "Fizz" in lieu of 5, 10, 15, 20, 25, 30, 35, 40, 45, all the numbers in the 50s, as well as 60, 65, 70, 75, 80, 85, 90, 95, and 100. (Since all numbers containing a 5 are multiples of 5, excepting the sequence from 51 through 59, Fizz is a little easier to play without messing up than is Buzz.)

And then there's Fizz-Buzz. More complicated, this game is a combination of Fizz and Buzz and involves "Fizz"ing on all the multiples of five or numbers that have a five in them, as well as "Buzz"ing on all the multiples of seven or numbers that have a seven in them. Thus: "One," "Two," "Three," "Four," "Fizz," "Six," "Buzz," "Eight," "Nine," "Fizz," "Eleven," "Twelve," "Thirteen," "Buzz," "Fizz," "Sixteen," "Buzz," "Eighteen," "Nineteen," "Fizz," "Buzz," "Twenty-two," and so on. "Fifty-seven" is "Fizz-buzz," and "Seventy-five" is "Buzz-Fizz." "Thirty-five" can be called either "Buzz-fizz" or "Fizz-buzz."

Again, the object in a non-competitive version would be to try to get to 100 without messing up. (And then, when someone messes up, to try to get the rest of the way to 100 without another slip. And then,

when another one occurs, to see how few mistakes you're going to make *now*, because surely now you've learned and will get it right!)

If the players start getting the hang of it, "Buzz"ing and "Fizz"ing at all the appropriate times, speed them up, increasing the tempo at which they call out their numbers, which will also increase the propensity for error.

BEEP!

Related to Buzz and Fizz, Beep! is a game that, like its relatives, can sometimes turn raucous with kids "Beep"ing loudly and laughing heartily. In Beep! the players recite the alphabet quickly, but each time they come to a vowel, instead of saying the vowel, they say "Beep!" (For the purpose of this game, Y, a sometimes-vowel, is considered to be one.)

MATERIALS NEEDED:
None

AGE OR SKILL LEVEL:
Knows alphabet and can differentiate vowels from consonants

The first player (two or more can play) leads off with "Beep!" (in lieu of "A"), followed by the second player saying "B," the third player (or the first, again, in a two-player game) saying "C," followed by "D," followed by "Beep!" then "F," "G," "H," and then "Beep!" again, and so on through the twenty-six letters.

In the non-competitive version of the game, players who goof are not eliminated. The object is simply to get through the alphabet without anyone making an error. Failing to substitute "Beep!" for a vowel—or "Beep"ing inappropriately, or calling out the wrong letter—is a mistake but carries no penalty or forfeit.

After getting through the alphabet once, the players can try it again at a faster pace—and faster and faster, till everybody's messing up because of the speed or till nobody's messing up because they've all gotten so good at it.

THE WORD OF THE HOUR

The Word of the Hour is one of those games that can grow into a perennially recurring source of family goofiness. The game can be played by virtually anyone of any age—well, old enough to talk—whether it's two kids, ten kids, or the whole family.

Someone chooses the Word of the Hour, and for the next hour—or ten minutes, or whatever time limit you set—every sentence uttered by every player must

MATERIALS NEEDED:
None

AGE OR SKILL LEVEL:
Four and up

have that word in it. If the word is "purple," every sentence anyone speaks must have the word "purple" in it. If the word is "frog," you're going to hear a lot of "frog"s for the next five minutes or half-hour or whatever.

It's better if the word chosen is a noun, adjective, or adverb, and it's better if you can work it into the sentence in a relatively meaningful or grammatically consistent way.

7

But whether the *purple* word is worked in in a natural way or an obvious one, each player should find a way to drop it into every sentence. There are no *purple* penalties for failing to do so, of course, but it's more fun if everyone succeeds. Every *purple* time.

Months after its first use in a game situation, the word will pop back up … not only during a *purple* game but just in casual conversation, referring to that especially silly game your kids played six weeks ago. This might even take place during some semi-momentous event, such as a phone conversation with Great-Grandma; it's hoped it would not occur during something more solemn, such as a recitation of wedding vows!

SUBSTITUTE NOUNS

Another required word game that can get wonderfully silly is Substitute Nouns. As with the Word of the Hour, certain word combinations will probably strike the players as so funny that they (the words, not the players!) survive beyond the game and pervade family conversations for months afterward.

MATERIALS NEEDED:
Paper and pen
or pencil

AGE OR SKILL LEVEL:
Seven and up

First each player makes up a list of five nouns but doesn't show them to the other players. Then each player writes five sentences. Virtually any sentence will do, though it's often funnier if some of the sentences involve other family members (or other friends, if your child is playing with friends rather than siblings). Short, simple, declarative sentences will do nicely: Mom really likes to eat steak. Janet has four new dolls. Dad drove to the store for doughnuts. I really want a new bike for my birthday. Hal taught Shep to sit up and beg.

Each player now passes his list of substitute nouns to the player on the left. The first player reads his first sentence aloud. Some people prefer to have the player read the sentence twice: once as written, then again with the first substitute noun on the list in place. Others like to skip reading the sentence the "right" way and go straight for the altered version. Your kids need to decide ahead of time which way they're going to play, and be consistent.

Let's say the substitute-noun list that was passed to Matt reads: shark, branding iron, space shuttle, pancake, schoolteacher. If he had written the five sentences above, they would now read: Mom really likes to eat shark. Janet has four new branding irons. Dad drove to the store for space shuttles. I really want a new pancake for my birthday. Hal taught the schoolteacher to sit up and beg. (Note that you can add a plural "s" at the end or an "a," "an," or "the" if needed to make the sentence grammatically correct.)

A MATTER OF PERCEPTION

This is an exercise that can teach a number of lessons, mainly that there is often no one "right" answer to a question such as "What happened?"

The next time the kids all watch the same movie (it doesn't matter if it's on cassette or in the theater) or TV show, ask them all to tell simply the story of the movie or show. If writing is too onerous a chore for them, or if one or more of them are too young to write and spell the words they'll need to express what they want to say, you can have them tell the story aloud. But

MATERIALS NEEDED:
None, or paper and pen or pencil

AGE OR SKILL LEVEL:
Four and up

writing is preferable, as each will have set down her thoughts before another child speaks, and no one will be influenced by what a sibling said first.

Stress to them that this is not schoolwork or a test. No one is going to be graded on his observations, and spelling and grammar don't count. They should just express, as completely as they can, the story of the movie or TV show.

When everyone has written her version of the story, each player should read hers aloud, one by one. Doubtlessly, one child will focus more on one aspect of the story and another on a different aspect. Even in reporting on the same happening within the story, one child may have a different perception of just what happened, or the motivation for it. Was Tom Sawyer being lazy, clever, or sneaky in trying to get that fence painted by someone else?

There are several lessons to be derived from this exercise, but perhaps the chief one is that there are various valid viewpoints in many situations. When Todd gives one version of a fight and Colin contradicts him, it's not necessarily true that one of them is lying. They may both have different but equally valid perceptions of what occurred.

And this, in turn, is because *people* are different from each other. Little kids expect others to react as they do, feel as they do, think as they do. This exercise shows them that not all minds work alike.

It shows them, too, that people have different viewpoints, and everyone is entitled to his or her point of view. You may not agree with mine, and I may not agree with yours, but we are each entitled to see things our way—and the fact that your way of thinking differs from mine doesn't necessarily make yours wrong.

The exercise may even make your kids more observant. Some details one child reports in a movie or TV show may be things another child overlooked altogether. ("I was so busy looking at the horse, I didn't even notice what the man was doing to the car.") It may also make them more thoughtful, as in a case when one child offers a reason for the behavior of a character, when another child just accepted the behavior at face value without considering why the character acted as he did.

RULES OF LIFE

Rules of life can be suggestions of how to live life or observations about the way things go. They can be serious but are best appreciated (like most things) when they're funny.

They might include:

MATERIALS NEEDED:
None, or paper and pen or pencil

AGE OR SKILL LEVEL:
Six and up

♦ The day you're out of school sick is always pizza day in the cafeteria.

♦ It always rains on Parents' Visiting Weekend at camp.

♦ Lending clothes is a good way to make bad friends.

♦ Doing your homework on the school bus isn't going to win you good grades for penmanship.

After offering the above examples to your kids, have them set about making their own rules of life—either aloud or on paper.

CREATIVE ALIBIS

Nobody loves being lied to, but everyone can't help admiring a creative liar just a bit. And if the untruth is forthrightly presented as just that, and nobody's *really* trying to fool anyone, then it's all really an exercise in creativity.

Your kids will probably enjoy showing off their most creative excuses for not accomplishing tasks in a timely manner. (And since you'll have heard their best excuses already, when they *really* need an alibi, they'll have nowhere to turn but the truth!)

MATERIALS NEEDED:
None

AGE OR SKILL LEVEL:
Five and up

So your challenge to them is to come up with the most creative alibis they can think of for the following:

- ♦ Why they didn't clean their room.
- ♦ Why their homework wasn't done in time.
- ♦ Why they haven't yet walked the dog/changed the gerbil's cage.
- ♦ How that grape jelly stain got on the armchair.
- ♦ Why George Washington chopped down the cherry tree.

A HANDSOME PRINCE AND I ATE STRAWBERRIES AND CHEESE ALL DAY LONG.

THE ___ FAMILY MEMORY BOOK

Of course you have a family photo album, and a picture is worth a thousand words, right? Not always. . . .

First of all, there are many special family memories that may not have been captured in pictures. Beyond that, pictures don't always tell the whole story. That picture of Jenny taking a bow at the end of the fifth-grade play may show how cute, or solemn, or impressive she looked, but it probably won't show how nervous she was beforehand. It may not show the daisy her best friend tossed up onto the stage at her. It surely doesn't convey the teacher's remark that Jenny was the best actor onstage that day. And, with her costume properly in place in the picture, there's little or no reminder of that terrible mix-up that almost kept the show from going on. (It was funny afterward but upsetting as heck at the time!)

There are memories associated with events that pictures of those events don't begin to convey. And what of all the events, big and small, for which no pictures were taken? The

MATERIALS NEEDED:
Paper and pen or pencil or typewriter, scrapbook or notebook, possibly decorations such as photos, construction paper and glue and scissors, or other at the kids' own discretion

AGE OR SKILL LEVEL:
Four and up

return of Susan's best friend for a visit after her family had moved to Idaho two years earlier. The day Dad and Alan reeled in that big fish together—there were no cameras to record the event, and they threw the fish back after catching it. The pie Mom baked for the school bake sale that she forgot to add sugar to—what picture could convey that, even if you'd taken one?

And not all memories are "big" memories—memories of major events. Many are of small events, or nonevents, that are still sweet or bittersweet, comic or sad, poignant or otherwise memorable. But they're still worth preserving—and they're likely to get lost over time.

Get it all down on paper before it gets away from you. If it's an event that more than one of you participated in, get all points of view—those of each parent and each kid who played a part in the happening, big or small. Let the kids choose memories, too. If you feel a certain item is worth preserving as a memory, by all means ask the kids, or those of the kids who were involved, to each contribute her own memories of it. But let them choose any other events of importance to them for recording in the memory book as well. We all have different memories, and we all have different values. If it's important to them, it belongs in the book even if it was a ho-hummer to you. This is a *family* memory book, not just yours.

Save those memories now, and do it together. Talking aloud as you write can help, too. Susan's saying that she remembers something about a dunk tank may be the spark to set off Jenny's memory of Dad dressing as a clown for Carnival. Alan's memory of the fish may remind Susan that she was along on that trip, too, and that Alan said or did something memorable that he and Dad may have forgotten till Susan reminded him. As one memory sparks another and you and the kids work harmoniously together, the memories will return and the book will grow.

And of course, going back over the book periodically provides another harmonious amusement the family can engage in together with no more competition than the occasional "It's *my* turn to read now."

CAUSE AND EFFECT

This is a game for two or three players. (If more than three want to play, the others have to sit out one round and participate in the next—each round is short, so there's not much waiting time involved.)

In a three-player game, Player 1 leads off with a fairly straightforward statement, such as, "I had peanut butter for lunch." Player 2 then has to give a cause for Player 1's statement—a silly cause. In the case of the example above, Player 2's cause might be, "Because the cafeteria was out of marshmallow casserole with moose gravy." Player 3 then has to give an effect, a result of the situation described by Player 1. In the example I've been using, Player 3's effect might be: "And he ate so much that he created a worldwide shortage of peanut butter."

MATERIALS NEEDED:
None

AGE OR SKILL LEVEL:
Seven and up

In a two-player game, Player 1 gives the original statement, Player 2 gives the cause, and then you go back to Player 1 for the effect.

In a four-player game, Player 4 sits out the first round. In the second round, Player 2 gives the original statement, Player 3 gives the cause, Player 4 gives the effect, and Player 1 sits out the round. With more than four players, the order would continue in a similar manner.

The game is over when each player has had a chance to start a round, but if everyone's still having fun, why not play another round, and another, and another…

BECAUSE YOUR MOTHER WANTED YOU TO BUY 10 CANS OF SPAM AND 50 PINTS OF ICE CREAM

I WANT TO SELL YOU A KANGAROO

This game is a good excuse for kids to indulge in pure silliness, but at the same time they'll be stretching those creativity muscles. Though a two-player game, three or more can play by taking turns. If Jeff, Janna, Mark, and Caitlin are playing, Jeff can be the seller and Janna the buyer for the first round. Then Janna's the seller and Mark's the buyer. Then Mark's the seller and Caitlin's the buyer, and finally Caitlin's the seller and Jeff's the buyer. In a two-player game, the players should simply switch off, with one buying and the other selling, then the two trading places for the next transaction.

Player 1 starts off with "I want to sell you a ____." The item "for sale" should be at least far-fetched if not outrageous. An oil well, a derrick, an igloo, a skyscraper, a feather duster, an ostrich, or the eponymous kangaroo are all good candidates for mention in this game.

MATERIALS NEEDED:
None

AGE OR SKILL LEVEL:
Seven and up

Player 2, exhibiting no sales resistance whatsoever, agrees to buy the object and gives a good reason for wanting to buy it—a reason that should be silly, funny, interesting, clever, or absurdly outrageous. In the case of the kangaroo, Player 2 might answer, "Oh yes, it would be great to have one around in the winter. It would keep me warm in its pocket on cold days," or "I'd like to buy your kangaroo. If I missed the school bus I'd have a way of getting to school."

That's the end of the round, and Player 2, having agreed to buy the kangaroo, now offers to sell something equally unlikely to Player 1, who has to give a reason for agreeing to buy it.

There's no formal end to the game. When the players run out of steam, and the answers stop being as clever, or funny, or good, then it's time to play something else.

FAMILY/FRIENDS MEMORY CHALLENGE

Though a challenge, this game isn't competitive. The kids are likely to love this game because so much of it centers around them: their memories, and other family members' memories, which are likely to involve them.

The premise is easy: Each player names an object, a place, or a color. (If you want, you can widen the game's horizons by including other categories as well.) Then, each player in turn has to offer a memory spurred by that word. If James starts, he might say "Blue." "Blue" might remind Ryan of the color of his bunk his first year at summer camp. He needs to say more than just, "My bunk at Camp Hiawatha was blue," but his memory needn't be longer than a few sentences. Then it's Liza's turn, and she might say, "Blue was the color of the van Mom and Dad rented for our trip to Grandma's. It was the first time we'd ever driven to her house instead of flying. I liked the restaurant where we stopped for lunch and played video games for an hour till the storm let up. I beat you six games out of eight, Ryan." (Ryan might not appreciate hearing *that*

MATERIALS NEEDED:
None

AGE OR SKILL LEVEL:
Five and up

memory very much!) Last it's James's turn to present a memory sparked by the word "blue."

Now it's Liza's turn to offer a word. She might say, "Lake Ronkonkoma," "a smooth stone," "our old house," "violet," "a dandelion," "papier maché," or _____? Then everyone again comes up with a memory connected to that word. And finally it's Ryan's turn.

The kids can elect to stop after everyone has had one chance at choosing a word to prompt memories, or they can play another round … and another…

Though better suited to families, the game can be played by close friends too, especially if they share a common history together (such as if they've all been in the same school and class for several years, and/or have been to the same camp together).

Younger kids are less interested in hearing memories that don't touch on them at all. But if the players are mature enough to be interested in each other's experiences that don't involve themselves, or if the players agree to refrain from using memories of places and people not known to the other players, the game can still be fun. The child who doesn't want to hear about his friend's aunt, whom he's never met, may be perfectly content to hear a memory about an incident that took place in his school, even though it didn't involve him.

And of course, the more details each child goes into with her memories, the more interesting the game's going to get.

EARLY MEMORIES

This works either in family groups or among friends. Kids love remembering back to the earliest times they can call to mind, or to special, if more recent, events.

Among a family group, if Kenny remembers a special birthday, a particular holiday celebration (like the year it snowed on Christmas), a family trip, or a visit from Grandma, Chrissy can chime in with tidbits she remembers that Kenny may have overlooked, and Stu can contribute his recollections as well.

Among friends, the topic may be "My Best Birthday," "The First Christmas I Can Remember," or "The Earliest Vacation I Remember." Slightly older kids can contribute "My First Night at Summer Camp," "My

MATERIALS NEEDED:
None

AGE OR SKILL LEVEL:
Three and up

First Day of First Grade," or "The First Time Mom Left Me Alone for Five Minutes." Each friend can contribute his or her own memory, which may not be of the same Christmas, school day, etc. as the other kids, though it can be if they were classmates back then, or went to the same camp, or were friends on the Christmas in question and got together to play with each other's new toys.

Of course, if the kids really get into the activity, they can create a Memory Book, writing down their recollections and preserving them for the future. But it is in no way necessary to get into anything that formal; just remembering aloud and sharing the memories with family and/or friends is enough.

THE ___ FAMILY DICTIONARY

In the tradition of *Family Words* [Paul Dickson, Addison-Wesley] and *Sniglets* [Rich Hall, MacMillan], your kids can create their own words and even compile a dictionary of them.

You may already have a few words that are peculiar to your family. Perhaps your family has always called the fuzz you find in pants cuffs "greyron," or maybe when your son was little he called keys "jinglies," and the name has remained in family usage.

To these family-coined words already in existence, the kids can add as many more words as they feel like inventing. They can be nonsense words whose sounds the kids like and for which they invent meaning. Or they could be words based in some logic: "greyron" derives in part from the grey color of the lint that lines pants cuffs, and "jinglies" certainly is evocative of the sound keys make when shaken.

But kids don't have to all be part of the same family to coin words for a dictionary together. All they have to be is imaginative, and unafraid of being a little silly. Instead of *The ___ Family Dictionary*, the undertaking might be *The Mark, Mike, & Ronnie Absurd Dictionary*, or *Lisa and Andrea's Excellent Dictionary*.

An excellent, absurd undertaking indeed!

MATERIALS NEEDED:
Paper and pen, pencil, or typewriter

AGE OR SKILL LEVEL:
Able to write

Ticking Bomb: Our parents' alarm clock

Spotrun: The pet door Spot, the dog, uses to go outside

The Spook House: The basement

DON'T MAKE ME LAUGH

Want to have a fit of the giggles? Try hard not to laugh. Want to make someone else have a fit of the giggles? I'm sure you know how … and I'm certain your kids do!

Two or more kids can have a lot of laughs—literally!—with this silly game. One tries to make another laugh, while the recipient of the mirth-provocation tries hard *not* to laugh—and tries to make his counterpart break out in giggles at the same time.

MATERIALS NEEDED:
None

AGE OR SKILL LEVEL:
Three and up

Of course, the harder you try not to laugh, the harder it is not to. With each participant engaged in making funny faces, telling jokes, or whatever else she feels will do the trick, and each participant trying not to laugh at the other's antics, pretty soon you'll have two (or more) kids holding their sides in laughter.

But watch out—laughter is contagious. You could catch it too!

THE WILD
BLUE YONDER

The U.S. Air Force, according to their song, takes off into the "wild blue yonder"—but so do your kids every time they engage in a session of daydreaming. Some parents discourage daydreaming as "useless" or "nonproductive." They think of it as the thing kids do when they should be studying, or when they "ought to" be out "doing something" (whether playing ball, or taking out the trash).

Granted, daydreaming isn't active. Granted, if a child is supposed to be studying he shouldn't be daydreaming. But to say a child who's daydreaming isn't "doing something" is to miss the point—he very much *is* doing something—he's stretching the creative muscles, and the imagination. And he may even be setting future goals for himself.

The child who daydreams about having a million dollars may well grab hold of a dream and pursue it, becoming a motivated adult who earns a decent dollar. The child who daydreams about helping unfortunate animals may daydream herself into a successful career as a vet. And the child whose daydreams don't lead anywhere in particular is still exercising his creativity and imagination, two very important "muscles."

So what sort of imaginings can you lead your children through? Kids really enjoy answering questions like the following ones, which each can give an answer to in turn. You probably don't want to throw all the questions at the kids in one session; save some for other days. And feel free to add questions of your own. (What your kids say in response may be instructive to *you*, if you're listening, too.)

MATERIALS NEEDED:
None

AGE OR SKILL LEVEL:
Five and up

- If you had a million dollars, what would you do with it?
- If someone gave you that same million dollars with the provision that you couldn't spend any of it on yourself, what would you do with it?
- What period of time would you like to visit if you could time-travel, and why?
- Suppose you could actually *live*, not just visit, in a different time—what era would you pick? Describe a day in your life in that time.

- If you could be any animal, what animal would you choose?
- If you had three wishes granted to you, what would you wish for?
- If you could be president for a day, what would you do?
- If you had the power to pass laws all by yourself, what laws would you pass?
- If you had one day to show a visitor from overseas around your town, what would you show her?
- If there were no changing seasons, what season would you like it to be all year, and why?
- If an alien spacecraft landed in the schoolyard, what would you do?
- If you were in charge of the school system, what changes would you make?

- What super-power would you most like to have, and what would you do with it?
- If you could redesign your house any way you wanted, how would you do it?
- Suppose you could redesign the human body—how would you redesign it?
- If you could have anyone else for parents, whom would you choose and why?
- If you could live anywhere you wanted, where would you choose?
- If you could be famous, what would you want to be famous for?

I'D LIVE WITH MY FAMILY IN FRANCE WITH LIONS AND LLAMAS AS PETS AND MY BEST FRIEND ANNA'S FAMILY LIVING WITH US, TOO.

A WISH LIST FOR THE WORLD

There are all kinds of creative daydreaming. Virtually all are non-competitive, but this one is a truly positive activity in that it gets the kids to thinking about what's wrong with the world and how it could be made better.

"A wish list for the world" is the topic of the fantasizing. Sit the kids down and ask them to dream up such a wish list. It might include such major items as:

MATERIALS NEEDED:
None, or possibly paper and pen or pencil

AGE OR SKILL LEVEL:
Five and up

- No disease
- No wars
- People of all races getting along in harmony and go on to include such lesser items as

    - A computer at every child's desk in school
    - Free toys for all kids regardless of their parents' finances as well as items that are strictly in the realm of fantasy, such as

- Year-round climate-control with no temperature extremes
- Moonlight as bright as sunlight so kids can go out to play after dinner in winter as well as summer.

You may need to give the kids an example or two from those suggested above, but let them be the ones to think of most of the items for their list on their own. The items for their wish list can be eminently sensible or fantastically outrageous. They can be wishes that could truly be attainable some day or wishes that are impossible to strive for but fun to fantasize about.

When the kids have come up with as long a list as they want to, possibly writing the wishes down on paper, you can ask them which of these items might be attainable and spark a discussion on how the members of the human race could go about turning some of these wishes into actual goals and achieving them.

WORD-AND-NAME CHAINS

Free association, according to Freud, was a means of learning what bubbled in the depths of a patient's psyche. But forget the psychological aspect—your kids can have fun seeing what name or word springs to mind in response to another. As one word sparks another, which sparks another, which sparks another, the kids are bound to come up with some amusing links in the chain. But even if none of the links is out-and-out hysterical, the game is fun and fast-paced. Here's a sample chain:

MATERIALS NEEDED:
None

AGE OR SKILL LEVEL:
Seven and up

Tom: "Light"
Lisa: "Bulb"
Tom: "Tulip"
Lisa: "Kiss"
Tom: "Chocolate"
Lisa: "Bar"
Tom: "Jail"
Lisa: "Crook"
Tom: "Arm"
Lisa: "Wrestle"
Tom: "Hold"

. . . and so on, till one of the kids gets stumped and cannot make an association to a word.

The object of the game is to keep the chain going as long as possible. In this, the game is cooperative. Players are not trying to stump the other player(s), and are not to try to think of names or other words that are going to be particularly difficult to associate to. There is no single winner or loser, but the players are all winners if they can make a particularly long chain.

Some pointers to note:

♦ Multiword combinations are permissible, such as "Twelve times twelve."

♦ If a player cannot think of an association, he is free to ask another player for help. No one drops out of the game.

♦ Two or more players—up to a whole partyful of kids—can play.

Any player who doesn't understand the connection between two words is free to ask how another player got from one word to another. But this is not a challenge, as there are no points awarded. It is merely a question.

If a player asks another player to explain a jump and there is no valid rationale for it, there are no penalties. The player should simply be asked to think of a different word or name instead. If she cannot come up with one, the other players can help. If the chain has truly come to a dead end, the game is over, in which case the players may want to start a new chain, or if everyone's tired of playing, it's time to play something else.

FAR-FETCHED CONNECTIONS

This is best played by three players but can also be played by two; and if more than three want to play, that's possible too, with all taking turns. But let's look at a three-player game as an example.

The premise is simple: Player 1 (we'll say that's Aaron) names a word. Player 2 (Sara) names an unrelated word. And Player 3 (Joey) has to find a way to connect them by some kind of logic, however circuitous or devious. If he succeeds, everybody wins. If not…try another set of words. But, whether or not Player 3 was successful, next time Sara is Player 1, Joey is Player 2, and Aaron is Player 3. Let's look at one round of the game:

Aaron: "Book."
Sara: "Office."
Joey: "When I go to my mom's office on a school holiday, sometimes I have to sit quietly and read a book."

Let's play another round. Now it's Sara's turn to start:
Sara: "Raccoon."
Joey: "Knife."
Aaron: "A raccoon building a dam might create a small fork in

MATERIALS NEEDED:
None

AGE OR SKILL LEVEL:
Eight and up

the river. And a fork and a knife are both utensils."

One more time? Now Joey leads off:
Joey: "Hat."
Aaron: "Ceiling."
Sara: "In a crowded house, with no closet space, you could hang long hooks from the ceiling to hang coats and hats from."

♦ In a two-player game, Sara would give the first word, Aaron would give the second, and the turn would go back to Sara to find the connection. Next round, Aaron would start, Sara would give the second word, then it's back to Aaron for the connection.

♦ In a four- (or more-) player game, Kayla would sit out the first round. Aaron would sit out the second round, while Kayla would move up into the Player 3 position, and so forth.

♦ There is no formal end to the game. Continue till the players are tired of the game and want to play something else, or it's time for dinner or for visiting friends to go home.

HEAD 'N' TAIL CATEGORIES

If you're familiar with the old game Geography, you know the mechanics (but not all the rules) of this game: If the first player's word ended in a "B," the second player's word has to start with a "B." But in Geography, two or more players are vying to stump each other. In this game, two or more players are trying to keep the game going as long as they can. And in Geography, players only call out geographical place names; in this game, the category, which is established at the beginning, can be countries, animals, flowers, birds, football players, cartoon characters, movie stars, rap singers, or virtually anything else.

Two or more can play. First the players need to agree on a category; let's say they choose animals. Shawna leads off with "Giraffe." Since her word ends (the "Tail" of the game's title) in an "E," Shane, who's next, has to supply an animal beginning (the "Head" of the game's title) with an "E." Perhaps he says "Elephant." This leaves Shawna (in a two-person game) or Jeffrey (in a three-person game)

MATERIALS NEEDED:
None, or possibly a watch, or paper and pen or pencil

AGE OR SKILL LEVEL:
Able to spell

with a "T"—which could be "Tiger," for instance.

If the next player says "Rhino," the following player might be stuck. But the game isn't competitive. If Shane can't think of an animal beginning with "O," he can say, "Help?" and Shawna can volunteer "Orangutan." Likewise, if Shawna then can't think of an animal beginning with "N," Shane is free to suggest "Newt."

It's not necessary to keep track of how well the players are doing; just keeping the game going as long as possible is good enough. But for kids who have the urge to compete, the game can be turned into a "personal best" effort, in which the players don't compete against each other but simply try to better their previous team record.

This can be done in any of several ways:

♦ Keep track of how many animals you've all thought of till the chain is broken. Now try another category—say, colleges—and try to beat your record for animals.

◆ Keep track of how many minutes you can keep the chain going, noting the time with a stopwatch, rather than counting actual numbers of items thought of. Then try to beat that record with your next category.

◆ Keep track of all your scores for one day: Animals—twelve (or five minutes), flowers—seven (or four minutes), Native American tribes, foods, TV shows, and so on. Then attack those same categories on another day and see if you can raise your scores over last time's efforts.

But I would like to stress that in no way is it necessary to time or keep track of the number of minutes or responses through which the game can be kept going. This is only an extra feature that can be added in the case of kids who are essentially competitive and, in the absence of a competitive game, want to try to beat *something*—in this case, their previous team record.

TELL ME A ME-STORY

Like many of us, kids' favorite topic of conversation is often themselves. Similarly, they love stories in which they star, too. What child wouldn't love to hear a tale in which she is the first astronaut on Venus, the cowpoke who tames the West, the citizen who helps the police catch the bad guys, or the child selected in a national talent show to star on the big screen (or on TV)?

So the next time the kids are looking for something to do, and you want a nice, quiet, non-competitive activity, suggest that they indulge in a round of storytelling . . . with themselves as the stars of the story.

Simply asking the kids to tell stories to each other may elicit groans, or requests of, "*You* read to us!" Asking them to make up stories for each other may bring blank expressions and protests of "I don't know what to tell about." But ask them to make up ficti-

MATERIALS NEEDED:
None or possibly pen or pencil and paper

AGE OR SKILL LEVEL:
Three and up

tious accounts of adventures that happened to themselves, or to each other, and you're likely to strike a spark.

You can keep the kids occupied for hours this way if you're lucky, each trying to make up ever-better stories about himself, or each telling stories of the other's derring-do in hopes the other child will be similarly complimentary to him.

This activity is equally as much fun for two kids, ten kids, or any other number, and it exercises the imagination while keeping the kids occupied non-competitively. You can specify that the kids should make up stories about each other, suggest they star themselves in the stories, require that the stories include both themselves and each other (practical for two or three kids but less so for a larger group), or leave it to the kids' discretion.

CHOCOLATE CAKE

The kids work together on this alphabet game that will net the winners a delicious prize. You, the adult, prepare for the game by writing on a piece of paper a treat you have at the ready for the kids. It might be CHOCO-LATE CAKE, ICE CREAM, APPLE PIE, or some other goodie, but whatever it is, you write the letters from top to bottom on the left side of the page, like this:

A
P
P
L
E

P
I
E

Now it is the kids' task to find, around the house, an item beginning with each of these letters. (In the example above they'll need three items beginning with P and two with E, along with one each of A, I, and L.) Though they can try to just think of appropriate items, they'll have an easier—and more

MATERIALS NEEDED:
Paper and pen or pencil

AGE OR SKILL LEVEL:
Able to write and spell

fun—time of it if they go around the house physically searching for suitable items to list.

If there's an apple in the kitchen, there's their A. If not, an antique clock, an apple peeler, an armoire, Aspirin, or an alphabet book all would do, and if they don't find any of the above items, they'll surely find something else. P could be the pie, sitting in the fridge, petunias or pansies growing on the windowsill, pants hanging in the closet, Pete, the family's Irish Setter, pots, pans, pancake mix ... well, you get the idea.

To make the game more complex and difficult, require that the items be listed *in order*. In other words, it won't do the kids a bit of good to find eggs in the fridge and list them till they have listed Ajax cleanser, pears, purse, and laundry hamper. Keep the list near where you are, and require that the kids come back to it and write down the items as they find them, rather than keeping the list with them as they roam the house. This will discourage fudging on the order of items, if you're playing a find-them-in-order version of the game.

When they've found one item for each required letter, they all get some of the treat.

Be careful what treats you select for this game; anything with letters that are difficult to find may prove too frustrating. For instance, FUDGE—of course the U could be underwear, but the kids might look right in their underwear drawers, see what they think of as "pants" or "panties," and never think of "underwear"—and there aren't too terribly many other U's in most houses. So gauge the age and thought processes of your kids before asking them to fill in the blanks for a treat that involves an X, Z, or possibly even U, or V. (With Victrolas a thing of the past, "vase" is your best bet for V, but if yours is a vaseless household, the kids may be in a bit of a jam—and I don't mean the grape variety.)

TONGUE TWISTERS

Tongue twisters are fun to try to conquer, and it's also fun to invent new ones. For starters, your kids can try their hands—or mouths—at three old familiar examples of the genre:

♦ She sells seashells by the seashore.
♦ The sixth sheik's sixth sheep's sick.
♦ Sister Susie's sewing shirts for soldiers.

How did your kids fare with those? Perhaps because they're familiar,

MATERIALS NEEDED:
None

AGE OR SKILL LEVEL:
Four and up

the kids have practiced and come close to mastering them. Great—let them try these new ones:

♦ Six slick sheep steal silently seaward.
♦ Save a single shaved cedar shingle.
♦ Simple Sybil's a swift civil servant.

When they've tired of these, let them try writing some tongue twisters of their own, trying them out as they go.

SECRET CODE LANGUAGE

What kid doesn't love secrets? What kid doesn't love being "in the know"? What kid doesn't love being able to shut out all the people who aren't in on something private?

No doubt you spoke Pig Latin when you were a kid—utbay ybay ownay ostmay idskay owknay owhay ootay eakspay igPay atinLay. So it's not a very satisfying secret code language.

Countless others have been developed over the years, though none as successful or universal as Pig Latin. Your kids—or your child and his or her friends—can develop their own

MATERIALS NEEDED:
Paper and pen or pencil

AGE OR SKILL LEVEL:
Six and up

secret code language. There's no formula for whomping up a secret code language—in fact, if there were, it would be easy for anyone else to decipher the language. But let them put their heads together and figure out, perhaps using Pig Latin as a model, a secret code language of their own.

Just figuring out the language together is a good cooperative activity, and of course they'll have lots of fun after that, speaking their language to convey Major Secrets to each other, or writing notes to each other in their secret code language.

CODED CAPERS

In quite the opposite of competition, a pair or group of kids who possess a secret code with which to send private, closely guarded, top-secret messages are working in the closest of cooperation. It's definitely "us against the rest of the world" instead of "you against me."

Granted the contents of these ultra-hush-hush missives aren't likely to threaten world stability. They're likely to run along the lines of "Isn't BethAnn (or Brad) cute?" or "I'll bet our history teacher flunked English." At most they might outline a bit of planned (and hopefully benign) mischief.

But if possession of a secret code unites your child and her friends in purpose and directs their energies in a cooperative manner, do you really care that they're planning a snowball attack on some kids from Ms. Hodgson's class after school? Or if the ability to send coded messages unites your own two kids, forestalling the usual squabbles and name-calling, how upset can you get over messages outlining plans for one child to distract you while the other slips the succotash to the family dog, positioned in advance under the table?

So how do your kids encode their private notes to each other? There are a variety of methods. Here are the three simplest systems:

MATERIALS NEEDED:
Paper and pen or pencil

AGE OR SKILL LEVEL:
Able to write and spell

Number-for-letter code:
Write the letters A through Z on two pieces of paper (or as many pieces of paper as there are to be kids "in" on the code). Below the A write 1, below the B write 2, below the C, 3, and so on till you reach Z and 26. The person sending the coded message refers to his code key, writing the numerals that represent the letters he needs to spell out the message. The recipient, referring to her copy of the code key, decodes the messages accordingly, translating a 4 as a D, and so on, recapturing the coded message.

Drop-a-letter code: This one almost doesn't need to be written out in a key, though doing so will save the mental gymnastics necessary for decoding. Simply, whenever you want to write an A, write a B. For an E, write an F. For a Z, write an A. The recipient of the note simply shifts gears, "translating" B back into A, N as M, G as F, and so on, to decode the message. (The reverse can also be used: The message is coded by turning B into A, A into Z, P into O, and so on. The decoder then shifts up one notch and decodes the message accordingly.)

Backward alphabet code: Write the alphabet out once, forward. Below those letters, write the alphabet backward. A = Z, B = Y, C = X, D = W, and so on. The disadvantage is that a semi-sophisticated code-breaker can figure this one out eventually. The advantage is that the principle is easy to remem-

ber; if a child loses his code key, it can be reconstructed easily.

With a code in place, your kids, or your child and his friends, can have hours of fun sending and receiving, coding and decoding, all sorts of super-private messages. Whether it's your daughter gossiping about boys with her friends, your son making plans to raid the Elm Street clubhouse and steal their flag, or your kids making plans together for a birthday surprise for you, they'll have lots of fun doing it—the more so just because of the mysterious nature of their writing. Everybody loves to have a secret!

DICTIONARY CHALLENGE

Admittedly this game is educational, and kids who balk at books won't have much fun playing Dictionary Challenge. "This isn't a game; it's more like schoolwork!" they're likely to protest.

But if you harbor in your household a child who's voracious to learn new words and who's good with language, have I got a game for her!

Each player roams through the dictionary, looking for interesting words that she thinks the other player doesn't already know. She writes five such words on a piece of paper.

After each player has complied her list, they exchange lists. Each player now looks up, in her dictionary, the five words she was handed on the list. After familiarizing herself with the meanings, she writes five sentences, each using one of the words. The two players then each read their five sentences aloud, defining each of the listed words as well.

MATERIALS NEEDED:
One each per player: dictionary, piece of paper, and pen or pencil

AGE OR SKILL LEVEL:
Eight and up

Working together, it is now the task of the two players to write ten new sentences that tell a reasonably coherent story, each of the ten sentences containing one of the listed words. The story doesn't have to be great literature, but it does have to have some sort of coherence and utilize each of the ten new words correctly, one per sentence.

Coati
Hooligan
Negligible

SPELLCHECK

If you skipped reading the previous game (Dictionary Challenge) as being unsuitable for your kids, pass this one by, too. But if your kids are the sort to enjoy an educational activity from which they can learn new words, they'll like this one. Some kids who like to play school enjoy Spellcheck, as well.

MATERIALS NEEDED:
One each per player: dictionary, piece of paper, and pen or pencil

AGE OR SKILL LEVEL:
Eight and up

As with the previous game, each player consults his dictionary and selects five words he's pretty sure the other player doesn't know. He then writes each word down, *deliberately misspelling it by one letter*, preferably not the initial letter.

Now the lists are exchanged, and each child looks up the five misspelled words he's been handed, a slightly daunting (but far from impossible) task, given that the spelling is incorrect. When he finds the correctly spelled word in his dictionary, each child needs to correct the spelling in writing on the paper and memorize the definition (without writing it down).

Let's say Jamie and Jordan are playing. Jamie starts, reading aloud the first word on her list, which Jordan misspelled. Jamie correctly spells the word aloud, after which *Jordan* is required to define it. (It was Jordan who selected the word from the dictionary—but does he remember what the word means?)

If Jordan does not remember the definition, Jamie can supply it. If Jamie, too, has forgotten, they need to look it up and refresh their memories.

Note that a word-for-word definition does not need to be parroted; a brief version of the dictionary's definition—or any one of the definitions, if there are several—will suffice.

The kids are now ten words richer in their respective vocabularies … and they're ready to look up five more words each and start all over!

DICTIONARY BLUFF

Here's another activity in a series of dictionary games for the language-oriented child who enjoys learning new words (see also Dictionary Challenge and Spellcheck).

Player 1 pages through the dictionary till she finds a word she thinks Player 2 doesn't know. She reads the word aloud and spells it.

Player 2 says either, "Yes, I know that word," or "No, I don't know that word." If he says he doesn't know the word, Player 1 reads it aloud, and both of them learn something. If Player 2 says he *does* know the word, Player 1 must decide whether to say, "I believe you," or "I think you're bluffing."

If Player 1 accepts Player 2's word that he knows the word in question, the dictionary now passes to Player 2. And if Player 1 attempts to call Player 2's bluff, and indeed Player 2 knows the word in question, the dictionary now passes to Player 2 as well. But if Player 1 calls the bluff, and Player 2 *is* bluffing, Player 1 retains possession of the dictionary for the next round.

MATERIALS NEEDED:
Dictionary

AGE OR SKILL LEVEL:
Eight and up

INERTIA.

A POISONOUS GREEN SNAKE WHO LIVES IN AFRICA.

DICTIONARY
ADD-ONS

This mirth-provoking game can be played by two or more players. For the sake of this explanation, let's say there are three players involved in a game. Choosing among themselves, they decide on the order in which they will play: Tina, Roy, and Mike.

MATERIALS NEEDED:
One dictionary

AGE OR SKILL LEVEL:
Ten and up

Tina opens the dictionary at random, and without looking she puts her finger down on a page. Whatever word or definition she has pointed to is the first word to be used in the game. That is, it doesn't matter if her finger lands directly on a word or some part of its definition; it is that word that will be used in the game. In this case, let's say her finger lands on "useless."

Roy must now supply a sentence using that word. He says, "It's useless to try to get 100 on Mr. Wainwright's social studies tests."

Roy now opens the dictionary at random, stabbing his finger at a word without looking. His finger has touched down on the definition of "sidewalk," so Mike must now fabricate a sentence employing *both* of the words, "useless" and "sidewalk." Mike says, "Glass is useless in making a sidewalk."

Now Mike opens the dictionary at random, points without looking at a word, and finds he has pointed to the entry for "imagine."

Tina must come up with a sentence involving "useless," "sidewalk," and "imagine." She says, "I imagine it's really useless to try to fry an egg on the sidewalk on a hot day, no matter what they say."

Play continues in this way till the players are tired of this string of words and are ready to start a new one, or the string gets so unwieldy that it's just impossible to craft a sentence. Then they start over with a new initial word and build up the string of add-ons from there.

ONE-FOR-ALL
SCRABBLE™

As with other games in this book, this game proves the point that many highly competitive games can be turned into cooperative, non-competitive games if both or all players play toward a common score. The purpose of the game then becomes to make that score as high as possible.

Toward that end, the two players sit alongside each other so each can see the other's seven tiles, which have been picked from the pool of tiles according to the usual rules of the game. The game proceeds from there according to the usual Scrabble rules.

The first difference in procedure, though, is that whatever score each player racks up is added to a common total. That is, if Kent and Carol are playing, there is only one column of

MATERIALS NEEDED:
Scrabble game

AGE OR SKILL LEVEL:
Able to spell

score being added up. Whether Kent or Carol makes the points, those points are added to the one running tally, which grows every time either player earns points.

The other difference is that the two players can see each other's board, and they work for each other's good. Carol, for example, looks for words she can lay down that will enable Kent to use his high-scoring "Z" in a strategically high-yielding square.

The higher the aggregate score at the end of the game, the better the two winners can feel about themselves.

REBUSES

YY U R
YY U B
I C U R
YY 4 me

If you figured out that the above actually says

Too wise you are
Too wise you be
I see you are
Too wise for me

then you can read a rebus.

And so can your kids, once they understand that the principle of a rebus is that letters, numerals, and simple drawings represent words or syllables. "Y" is "why," a picture of an eye is "I," "U" or a picture of a female

MATERIALS NEEDED:
Paper and pen or pencil

AGE OR SKILL LEVEL:
Able to spell

sheep (ewe) is "you," "2" is "to," "two," or "too." A "4" can mean "for," "four," or "fore." "B4" is "before." A picture of an oar is "or." "I C" is "I see" and "N M E" is "enemy." A picture of a hand, followed by an "E" is "handy."

With these principles in mind, your kids can create their own rebuses. They have a choice: They can literally work on creating the rebuses together, or each can create her own rebus, then they can exchange them and try to figure out the other's puzzle.

THE R&D DEPARTMENT

One of the things a Research & Development department does in a big corporation is find new uses for old products. New uses for old widgets? Why not?! It's a valid concept—and one that can be put to use with your kids, too!

Your challenge to the kids is to come up with new uses for specific items you'll mention to them. These don't have to be practical, they just have to make some sense. If corporate America isn't waiting on your doorstep with check in hand, that's fine—your kids are having fun. Here's an example: "How many new uses can you think of for a baseball cap?"

MATERIALS NEEDED:
None

AGE OR SKILL LEVEL:
Four and up

WHAT'S ANOTHER USE FOR A TOOTHBRUSH?

TO BRUSH MY DOLLY'S HAIR.

"A combination of perch and transportation for my parakeet on a sunny day—he can ride on the bill of the cap and see the world as I walk around the block."

"If my team loses the pennant, I can always let Mom use the cap as a planter. She's got a couple of plants that would fit in it."

"Soldiers could wear them with mirrors attached to the tops of the bills. They reflect the sunlight into the enemy's eyes and the enemy can't see to shoot at our guys."

You see, the uses don't *really* have to be practical. They can be down-to-earth or far-flung. All they *have* to be is creative.

TINY SHOE

In this game, everyone participates in thinking of uses for familiar objects that have been shrunken or blown up several times their usual size. For instance, one player says, "A tiny shoe." Now everyone else has to think of uses— sensible or preposterous— for a tiny shoe. Some suggestions might include "A doll's shoe," "A planter for a miniature cactus," and "A paper clip holder."

If, on the other hand, the object is "A giant mirror," suggestions for its use might be "Ice skate on it," "Reflect the sun in winter to make the weather warmer," or "Hang it on the fence of a small yard to make the yard look bigger."

Everyone should take a turn in suggesting the object for which uses are to be thought of. Naturally, since there's no scoring, everyone doesn't have to have exactly the same number of turns, but it's not fun and not fair if Allison is always the one to think of the next object.

MATERIALS NEEDED:
None

AGE OR SKILL LEVEL:
Four and up

INVENTIONS

Another realm of fantasy you can spin the kids off into is coming up with new inventions. This can be merely a matter of "Wouldn't it be nice if someone would invent a machine that makes the bed for you," or "What we need is a thermometer you could slip in your parents' mouths when they get home from work that would tell you what kind of a mood they're in and whether to let them cool down before you show them your report card." Or they could think of more practical, more plausible inventions.

MATERIALS NEEDED:
None or paper and pen or pencil

AGE OR SKILL LEVEL:
Four and up

"Inventions" don't have to be gadgets, either, or anything nearly that complicated. Inventions can be:

♦ A new flavor of ice cream (the kids should come up with a name for it as well as a description)
♦ A new food
♦ A new trick dogs can be taught
♦ A new toy
♦ A new type of clothing, as different from what an American child of this era wears as are space suits, kilts, saris, or loincloths
♦ A new game

As you can see, some of the items above your kids might actually be able to invent. A new game surely could be within their abilities to dream up. And a new ice cream flavor—complete with name—is something they can come up with even if they don't literally formulate the recipe. A new food dish may be well within their abilities, and depending on their ages they may even be able to experiment in the kitchen, perfect the recipe, and serve it for dinner or lunch one day.

But that's not to say they should avoid the realm of the more fantastic. Just because they can't figure out how to physically create the invention, or because it's one that's not likely to ever be practicably perfected by anyone, is no reason for them not to invent in theory, at least, a machine or other gizmo that can do fantastic things. Here are some possibilities:

♦ A machine that uses sound waves to keep a softball suspended in midair for batting practice by kids playing alone
♦ A machine that will take existing objects and enlarge them in real life, blowing up three-inch dinosaur

models to lifesize with the push of a button

♦ Sneakers with scoops attached, for playing "scoopball," in which the ball is never touched with the hands, only with the scoops

♦ A new kind of exercise equipment

Your kids can dream up names for all their gizmos, too. Remember the thermometer that measures parents' moods? You could call it a temperamenturameter!

Who knows? You may even be harboring a *real* inventor in the family, and this exercise might be just the thing to set his feet along the path to adult discoveries.

Hey, we don't need any life-sized tyrannosaurs in our back yards—not even plastic ones—but the world is probably ready for some new exercise equipment!

DESCRIBING PAIRS

This great cooperative activity for two players is especially suited to the younger set. This game develops language skills and descriptive abilities, and improves communication.

Start by selecting a category for your pictures—it could be men, women, kids, animals, houses, or any other category that you can find at least four pictures of in your magazine or newspaper. Cut out four or so identical pairs that all belong to your category. For example, you might find four pictures of different women in a magazine, and then cut out the same four pictures from your duplicate copy of the magazine, forming four sets of identical pairs.

Paste the pictures on cardboard. The size of the pieces of cardboard should be uniform, even if some of the pictures are much smaller than the size of the cardboard.

Break up the pairs so each of the two players has one of each picture, and shuffle the two piles. Now each child draws one picture without letting the other child see it.

MATERIALS NEEDED:
Two identical copies of a newspaper or magazine

AGE OR SKILL LEVEL:
Three and up

One child describes the picture she's holding, and the other child asks as many questions as he wants about it: "Is the woman wearing a green dress?" or "What color shoes is the man wearing?" or "Does the bicycle have a basket between the handlebars?"

If they don't think they are holding matching pictures, either of the kids can replace her card in her pile and draw another card, starting over with the inquiries. When they feel they are holding a pair, they both place their cards face up on the table. If they are right, they leave them in the middle of the table, pick another card each, and start all over. If they are wrong, they both return their cards to the bottom of the deck, pick the top card, and then shuffle.

Now they begin the process all over. But this time, the child who was answering the questions does the asking, and vice versa. When they have paired all the cards, the game is over and they have won.

POWERS OF PERCEPTION

This activity can be engaged in with familiar or unfamiliar objects. There are several variations of it, but let's take one: Two kids play, competing against only themselves, not against each other. Each tries to better her own score from the previous round, playing five rounds each.

Let's say Maria and Renee are playing. Maria shows Renee a familiar object: the living room sofa. Renee has thirty seconds to study it from as many angles as she wants. She then has to turn her back to it and make as many notes as she can about it. They all have to be facts, not memories or stories pertaining to the couch.

MATERIALS NEEDED:
Familiar objects, paper and pen or pencil

AGE OR SKILL LEVEL:
Able to write

- It's blue.
- It has paler blue threads running through it.
- It has four throw pillows.
- It has three cushions.
- It has "buttons" in the middle of each cushion.
- It has an old jelly stain on the end cushion.

If that's all Renee can think of—you can play with a reasonable time limit, such as two minutes, or you can leave it open-ended—she now stops writing, gives herself a point for each fact she noted, and turns back. She and Maria now go over her notes. Both of them should note any errors or omissions:

- It has brown legs.
- There is also a grease stain.
- The pale threads running through it are silver, not light blue.

Deduct a point for each incorrect observation. The net score is her score for round one.

Maria now picks another object for Renee to study, and she goes through the same procedure. Her objective is to get a higher score this time than before by being more observant and attentive to details. All told, she studies, turns her back on, and makes notes on five different objects. Then it's Maria's turn.

Now Renee picks five objects, one at a time, for Maria to study, familiarize herself with, and describe one point at a time. As before, Maria and Renee will go over Maria's list, noting errors or omissions. The object is *not* for Maria to best Renee or vice versa, but for each player to improve *her own* score each time, so that by the fifth round she has the highest score yet.

- Note that all five objects should be either familiar or unfamiliar, not a mix of each. It *is* a good idea, though, for one player to describe all familiar objects and the other player to describe all less-familiar objects. This makes the two players' efforts less comparable and discourages any tendency for the two players to compare their scores against each other and become competitive: "My final score was a 12 and you only got an 8." If the two are engaged in dissimilarly easy tasks, there's less likelihood of their competing with each other. *The competition is strictly to improve one's own "personal best." It is* not *against the other player.* In fact players could collaborate—both studying an object and then compiling a list together, then trying to improve next time.

THREE-AT-A-TIME STORIES

In this challenge to kids' ingenuity, a story is told by each player giving only three words at a time. As few as two can play, and the more the merrier.

Player 1 might start, "A boy named," leaving it to Player 2 to continue "Jerry had a," leaving Player 3 (or Player 1 again, in a two-player game) to add "pet hamster named" Then player 4 chimes in with "Rooster. Rooster was" Player 5: "a very clever" And so on.

When the story comes to a logical conclusion, the game is over. There's no requirement that everyone have a set number of turns. And when the kids get tired of the game, you can be sure someone will wrap up the story very quickly.

MATERIALS NEEDED:
None

AGE OR SKILL LEVEL:
Five and up

VERY SHORT STORIES

This is a game for two, three, or six players. Here's how two would play:

Player 1 writes the name of a male near the top of a piece of paper. The male may be adult or child, living or dead, real or fictitious, but should be a familiar name to both players. It might be Donald Duck, Dad, sixth-grade teacher Mr. Williams, or George Washington. Player 1 then folds the paper down just enough to cover the name and passes the paper and pen to Player 2.

Player 2 then writes "met" and the name of a female. Having no idea who the male in the story is, she may write "Cinderella," "Queen Elizabeth," "Shari Lewis," or your next-door neighbor.

After folding the paper again, she passes it back to Player 1. He, having no idea who the female in the story is, writes "at" or "in" or "on" and then a location—"at the spring dance" or "on the moon" or "on Main St." or "in the bathtub" or "in the Williams's station wagon" or "in Grandpa's back yard."

Once again the paper is folded and passed. Player 2, who knows who the female is but not who the male is, writes "He said," and then attributes a quotation to the unknown male. "He said, 'How about marrying me?'" or "He said, 'The dandelions are in bloom.'" or "He said, 'I flunked my math test.'"

The paper is again folded and passed, and—you guessed it—Player 1 writes "She said," followed by a quotation attributed to the unknown female.

Once again the paper is folded and passed to Player 2, who writes "So they" and follows it up with an action: "went skiing," "had ten kids," "were crowned king and queen of Never-Neverland," "took a bath," "jumped over the rainbow."

Then the paper is passed back to Player 1, who unfolds it and reads the "short story" aloud.

For a three-player game, the order is changed slightly:

Player 1: male's name
Player 2: "met (female)"
Player 3: "in/at/on ___"
Player 1: "She said, '____'"
Player 2: "He said, '____'"
Player 3: "So they _____"

MATERIALS NEEDED:
Paper and pen or pencil

AGE OR SKILL LEVEL:
Able to write

52

And for a six-player game, the order can be either "He said" first or "She said" first, so long as it's agreed upon ahead of time, so you don't wind up with two people writing "he" quotes, or two people writing "she" quotes.

It's a fun game with absolutely no competition—unless it's between two kids running to see who's going to get to the bathroom first, because they're both about to wet their pants from laughing so hard at the results!

MANGLED PROVERBS

It's fun to play with proverbs. At an early age, kids tend to take them literally. Later, as they get older, they understand that the proverbial "rolling stone" or "early bird" aren't really stones or birds, but it's hard to avoid thinking of them that way. Which leads to many mangled proverbs that get that way through honest error. But it's also fun to mangle a few on purpose.

The idea is to complete the first half of an old proverb in a way that either twists the meaning or takes the words more literally:

The early bird . . .
. . . will get awfully sleepy by two o'clock.
A rolling stone . . .

MATERIALS NEEDED:
None or possibly paper and pen or pencil

AGE OR SKILL LEVEL:
Six and up

. . . could hit somebody in the foot.
Marry in haste . . .
. . . to claim another dependent on this year's taxes.
People who live in glass houses . . .
. . . must spend lots of money on drapes.
A stitch in time . . .
. . . can keep your space-ship from going through a time warp.

Read one or two of the above examples to your kids, to give them the idea, then give them a few to complete on their own, or just ask them to complete some without hearing the examples first. Ask them to complete the proverbs in a way that makes sense to them, regardless of the original meaning.

I can practically guarantee that you'll have even more fun with the results than they will in dreaming them up.

SPOONERISMS

Tongue-tied 19th-century clergy-man W. A. Spooner, a frequent victim of his own slipping tongue, gave his name (how-ever inadvertently) to this particular brand of tongue-twistedness. It's the result of transposing a part of one word—usually the initial sound—onto another word, and vice versa.

Among the better-known examples are, "Let me sew you to your sheet" for "Let me show you to your seat," or "Mardon, me Padam," for "Pardon me, Madam," or "a blushing crow" for "a crushing blow."

Kids create spoonerisms naturally, without intention and without guile. But they love the sound of this particular type of merry mix-up and often will create deliberate, if ersatz, spoonerisms if the activity is suggested to them.

The game needn't be confined to the creation of comic mispronunciations of isolated pairs of words. Let them spin out a story frosted with the sweet delicacy of "twung-tisted" words whose initial sounds have been "momically kixed-up." They'll be tripping over their

MATERIALS NEEDED:
None

AGE OR SKILL LEVEL:
Five and up

own tongues as purposefully as a slapstick comic trips over his own two feet.

In fact, if they're typically tickled over the mixed-up words, don't be surprised if they go around for the rest of the day inverting word sounds, deliberately asking you "Dot's for winner?" and "Are there any frownies in the bridge?"

MY DOG JAKE HAS FROWN BUR.

"I ONE IT"

No, not "I won it"—this *is*, after all, a book of non-competitive games—but "I one it." That's the second sentence of this silly game that kids have been tricking other kids with at least since I was a child, and probably back to George Washington's day or earlier.

The first child says, "There's a chocolate cake on the table. I one it. Now you say 'I two it'."

"I two it," the second child says, obligingly.

"I three it," the first child replies, pointing at the second child, if necessary, to cue him.

"I four it," the second child replies.

"I five it."

"I six it."

"I seven it."

MATERIALS NEEDED:
None

AGE OR SKILL LEVEL:
Able to count to eight

"I eight it."

At which point the instigator counters with, "You ate it? You ate a whole chocolate cake all by yourself? You hog!" Or words to that effect.

Instead of the benign chocolate cake, the item the second player "eight" might be a bucket of mud, a scoop of slime, or a dead fish.

Kids in the Northwest, according to a friend, sometimes reply to "I eight it" with "and it's covered with maggots." Friendlier junior Northwesterners make a harmless joke out of "I eight it" by simply adding, "and there's a quart of peppermint ice cream with it," alluding to the fact that "I eight it" sounds like "I ate it" without accusing their friends or siblings of gross hoggery or the ingestion of vile substances.

FORTUNATELY

Unfortunately, I had never read *Fortunately* (Remy Charlip, Four Winds Press). Fortunately, Sheryl Pease had, and had devised this game based on the book. Unfortunately, I couldn't find a copy in my library. Fortunately, Sheryl explained to me how to play. . . . Do you get what I'm leading up to?

One player leads off, making a statement such as "Unfortunately, it had snowed when I got up the morning the circus was due in town." The next player starts her statement with "Fortunately"— "Fortunately, I had a sled on which to travel to the circus." The next player: "Unfortunately, I had no horses to pull the sled." Next player: "Fortunately, it was a straight run downhill to the circus."

"Unfortunately, when my mom got on the sled with me, it was too much weight for such a slight hill, and the sled didn't go anywhere."

"Fortunately, our dog is a St. Bernard, so I hitched him up to the sled."

"Unfortunately, when we got to the circus they said, 'No dogs allowed!' and we weren't willing to leave him tied up outside."

"Fortunately, Mom was carrying a bi-i-i-i-ig satchel with her, and we stuffed the dog inside."

And so on it goes, till the story comes to a logical end or just peters out, or the players have had enough and want to start a different story or play something else.

MATERIALS NEEDED:
None

AGE OR SKILL LEVEL:
Four and up

UNFORTUNATELY, SCHOOL WAS GOING TO END THREE WEEKS LATE FOR SUMMER VACATION.

FORTUNATELY, WE'LL BE PLAYING SOFTBALL EVERY MORNING.

HIGH DICE

Although kids of any age who are able to add to 100 can enjoy this game, kids in need of practice in addition will actually derive a benefit from it. Two or more can play; the pair (or group) take turns rolling the dice and adding up the score of everyone's dice rolls together.

The object of the game is to reach an *exact* number that has been predetermined; 100 is suggested as a goal the first time your kids play. Choose too low a number and the game is over too quickly; too high a number and the game drags on too long.

Player 1—let's say that's Laurie—rolls the dice first. She gets a 7 and writes that down on a piece of paper. Player 2—who we'll say is Kyle—rolls an 11 and writes that down, adding it to the existing score and getting a total of 18. Now Laurie rolls again (assuming only the two are playing). She gets a 3, writes it down, and adds to get a total of 21.

Play proceeds this way, getting ever nearer the goal of 100. If the kids have a total of 93 and Laurie rolls an 8,

MATERIALS NEEDED:
A pair of dice, paper and pen or pencil

AGE OR SKILL LEVEL:
Able to add to 100

that would put them over 100. They have lost the game. (But if she gets a 5, the total is now 98 and Kyle rolls, hoping for a 2.)

If at any point the score stands at 99, only one die is rolled on the next turn.

Variations:

♦ Once within six points of goal, players stop rolling two dice and roll only one die instead.

♦ If the players are close to 100 (or whatever their goal is) and roll dice in excess of what they need to reach their goal, they have not automatically lost. They get three tries in which they can roll an excessive number and disregard it before the game is declared lost. If, within those three tries, they can roll the number that puts them at their goal, they have won.

NON-COMPETITIVE
DOUBLE SOLITAIRE

In this version of double solitaire, the players help each other rather than compete with each other. You'll need a large table, or else you'll want to play on the floor, as the players lay their cards out side by side.

I'm assuming you're familiar with the rules for the basic, standard form of solitaire, in which the object of the game is to play all the cards onto the aces at the top of the game. In this version, the players are free to play their cards onto any of the eight ace-based piles at the top of the layouts.

None of the piles "belongs to" one player rather than the other; if Marty has a five of diamonds and there is a four of diamonds showing on an ace-based pile above Greg's layouts, Marty is perfectly free to play his five there.

There is no competition in this game, no way in which either player can "beat" or "be ahead of" the other player. If both players succeed in emptying their lower piles and their decks, and building up the eight ace-based piles to

MATERIALS NEEDED:
Two decks of cards, preferably with different backs

AGE OR SKILL LEVEL:
Five and up

completion, the team has won. If either player does not succeed in getting rid of all his cards onto the top piles, then the team has lost even if one player has succeeded in ridding himself of all his cards. The object of the game is to achieve a complete, cooperative success.

After the team has reached either success or frustration, the decks need to be separated before the game can be played again. That's the reason it's preferable to have different backs on the two decks; it's easier to separate them that way.

59

MYSTERY GUEST

One player is chosen as the Mystery Guest, and she chooses an identity. This can be a real or fictitious person, living or dead. It can even be an animal—Lassie, Bugs Bunny, Alvin the chipmunk, Flipper. The person (or animal) chosen does not have to be of the same gender as the player—Nancy, who is playing the Mystery Guest, can choose to be Rip Van Winkle if she wants.

The other player is the Host. The Host interviews the Mystery Guest, as if she were a guest on a TV show. The Host asks the Mystery Guest any question (other than "Who are you?") that is not answerable just by yes or no. It might be, "When were you born?" or "When did you die?" or "Did you write many best-selling books?" or "Have you ever won an Oscar?" The questions should require some information of the Mystery Guest that will help the Host decide who the Mystery Guest is.

MATERIALS NEEDED:
None

AGE OR SKILL LEVEL:
Four and up

The Mystery Guest may answer questions evasively if she wishes, but she may not answer dishonestly. If she honestly doesn't know the right answer to a question, she must answer to the best of her knowledge. ("When were you born?" "I don't know exactly, but in the early 1800s.") However evasively she answers, eventually something will clue the Host in as to who his Mystery Guest is. At that point, the Host says, "Are you _____?" If he's right, the game is over. If the Host is wrong, the game continues till he gets it right (or gives up).

Then they switch places, with the player who was the Host becoming the Mystery Guest and vice versa.

Notes:

♦ In most cases, the Host will guess the identity of the Mystery Guest, so this is not really a competition to see if the Mystery Guest can stump the Host.

♦ The players are not to keep track of how many questions it takes the Host to guess the Mystery Guest's identity. This is not a competition to see who can get it in the fewest guesses.

♦ You can play with more than two players, the others being panelists. The Host and panelists should each ask one question at a time in turn, either going clockwise or in some other orderly fashion. This will help prevent each player from trying to guess the Mystery Guest's identity ahead of the others and turning the game into a competition.

FAMOUS PAIRS

The kids can work together on completing the following list of pairs, of which you'll supply only the first half, leaving it to them to supply the missing half. (I've given you the missing half in parentheses to settle any possible disputes.) You'll need to recopy the list, minus the answers, on a sheet of paper. Then let the kids work together on filling in as many of the blanks as they can.

MATERIALS NEEDED:
Paper and pen or pencil

AGE OR SKILL LEVEL:
Nine and up

Adam & ___ (Eve)
alpha & ___ (omega)
Antony & ___ (Cleopatra)
Army & ___ (Navy)
bag & ___ (baggage)
bed & ___ (board)
bed & ___ (breakfast)
black & ___ (white)
bow & ___ (arrow)
brush & ___ (comb)
cheese & ___ (crackers)
cup & ___ (saucer)
day & ___ (night)

ebb & ___ (flow)
near & ___ (far)
fine & ___ (dandy)
gold & ___ (silver)
Jack & ___ (Jill)
nuts & ___ (bolts)
salt & ___ (pepper))

When the kids have finished filling in as many of the missing pairs as they can, ask them to see how many more well-known pairs they can come up with.

62

ODD COUPLES

Any child old enough to write is old enough to play this game, and any number from two up can play. It helps if the players have a commonality of experience—this is a better game for friends, relatives, or schoolmates to play, rather than kids who are just getting to know each other.

MATERIALS NEEDED:
An even number of small pieces of paper, a pen or pencil for each player

AGE OR SKILL LEVEL:
Able to write

Each player is going to contribute names to each of two piles, one of male names and one of females. Pick a number of names that each child will contribute to each pile. For two kids playing, you might want each of the two to contribute ten names to each pile. For more than two kids, fewer names are advisable.

The names should be recognizable to all players. They can be names of people real or fictitious, living or dead, adult or child. They can even be anthropomorphic animals, such as Smokey the Bear or the Roadrunner. Just make sure that there's no confusion as to which pile of names is the females and which is the males. Each player contributes the same number of names to each pile, folding the piece of paper twice after writing on it, to be sure the name isn't visible.

When all players have contributed their names to both piles, each player takes a turn picking one name from each pile, unfolding them, and reading them aloud, matching up a male and a female. Player 1 might pick Wile E. Coyote and Grandma. Player 2 might pick Huck Finn and Susie, Player 1's sister. Player 3 might find he has paired up Ms. Whitman, the school's music teacher, with Kevin, the Cub Scout leader.

What fun to find a player's older sister has been matched with the jerkiest kid on the block, or a player's brother's girlfriend has been matched with the Abominable Snowman.

When all the names have been matched up, they can be refolded for another round, or they can be discarded and a new set of names written out.

TELL ME MY FORTUNE

A "fortuneteller" isn't always a Gypsy in a caravan, or a woman in a dark backroom who reads tea leaves. A fortuneteller is also the name for a little device kids have been making out of paper for generations.

With a pair of scissors, cut an 8-1/2 x 11" piece of paper so it's square. Now fold the four corners in toward the middle so the points all just meet; the result is a smaller square. Turn that square over and fold the four new corners in toward the middle. Press on all the creases so they're sharp and stay folded.

You now have a still smaller square, with four triangles facing up. (This is hard to envision, but if you'll make a sample fortuneteller as you read the instructions, you'll find it's easy to follow along.) Fold the paper twice more as follows:

Fold it in half from top to bottom, with the flaps remaining on the outside. Now return it to its previous condition before that fold. Now fold it in

> **MATERIALS NEEDED:**
> Paper, scissors, pen or pencil, possibly crayon

> **AGE OR SKILL LEVEL:**
> Able to write

half from left to right, again with the flaps remaining on the outside, and again return it to its previous condition. It should now be more flexible and more easily manipulated. You should again be looking at a small square with four triangles on the top of it.

Each of those four triangles is in a sense divided in half by the previous folds in the paper. If you look at it that way, you can think of the triangles as being composed of two segments each. So you are looking at eight segments. Write a number on each of the eight segments. You should use the numbers one through eight, but they do not have to appear in order. Unfold the paper, and under each half of each triangular flap, write a short fortune. (Short is all that will fit, even with small writing.) You will have eight fortunes when you're finished.

Now turn the fortuneteller over, so you are looking at the square side, with four smaller squares on it. On each of these square flaps write the name of a different color, or draw a stroke of a different color with crayon on each of the flaps. (If any of the players is colorblind, it'll be better to write the color names than to use crayon.)

Each child can make her own fortuneteller, and use it on the other kids. Here's how:

Slip each thumb and each forefinger under one square flap each. Slide your fingers all the way into the corners of the flaps and hold your fingers together, so that all that's visible is the four square flaps with the colors on them, not the inner flaps with the numbers on them.

The person whose fortune is about to be told chooses any one color from the four. Say he chooses orange. The operator of the fortuneteller holds her thumbs together and her forefingers together, but pulls her left fingers away from the right fingers, so the fortuneteller is open to four of the inner numbers. As she does, she says "O." Then, pressing right thumb and forefinger together, and left thumb and forefinger together, she allows the two thumbs to part and the two forefingers to part. As she does this, she says "R." Returning her fingers to their previous position, she says "A." She continues

spelling the color, moving her fingers as she does so, till she reaches the "E."

At this point four of the eight numbers are showing. The person whose fortune is being told now must choose one of those four numbers. Say he chooses seven. The operator now goes through the same manipulations with the fortuneteller, holding the one pair of sides together as she says "One," then holding the other pair of sides together as she says "Two," and so on up to "Seven."

When she says "Seven," four numbers will again be showing. The other person now chooses one of those four numbers, and the operator removes the fortuneteller from his/her hands and lifts up the flap under that number. Whatever's written underneath is the other person's fortune:

"You will have six kids."

"You will be rich and famous."

"You will be a great astronomer."

"You will write five best-selling novels."

… or whatever might have been written beneath those flaps.

Now the kids trade off, with the previous operator having her fortune told according to the other child's fortuneteller.

Of course, more than two can play. If there are five kids, each of the five can make a fortuneteller and tell the fortune of each of the others. It's not very scientific—in fact, I'd be amazed if many of the predictions came true!—but do you really think the horoscopes printed in the daily paper are any more fact-based?!

WHICH LETTER WINS?

Which letter appears most often in print—or at least, in a given printed passage? There are several ways your kids can go about this activity, but probably the simplest is for them to decide what they think are the likeliest letters, then count the number of times those letters appear on a given page or in a newspaper story, or even one short paragraph.

For kids with really analytical minds—you know if you have one!—it's possible to make a chart listing every letter of the alphabet, count the occurrences of every letter on two pages of a small-type book (or the whole of an easy reader), and determine which letter appears the most often.

For the average child, it's enough if each of the two, (three, four, or however many) kids counts the occurrences of a certain letter. Are there more E's than S's? More K's than D's? Or take the less-common letters and count them. Ever wonder if there are more X's than Q's in the average page of newsprint? More Y's than W's?

Highly competitive kids could turn even this pastime into a competitive contest. ("I say there are more F's." "I say there are more H's." "Well, we'll see who's right! I bet I am!") But if you have them agree on which two (three, four) letters are the most common, then have them look for those letters without anyone predicting which one will occur the most often, without anyone championing any given letter, you can take the potential competition out of the activity, defusing it from possible squabbles. The competition, then, is strictly among the letters, not among the kids.

MATERIALS NEEDED:
Book, magazine, or newspaper

AGE OR SKILL LEVEL:
Able to recognize letters and count them as they appear on a page

CAPTIONS OUTRAGEOUS

Y ou know that picture of your daughter that you never put into the photo album because she moved her arm when the shutter clicked? You know the picture of the two of you in which your head is partly cut off? The picture of Cousin Ed in which he was making such a funny face? And the picture of your son that was overexposed?

None of them made it into the album ... what a waste! Well, weep no more—I have a good use for them.

It's a project your kids can work on together harmoniously. They can literally collaborate on it, or they can work side by side individually, comparing notes as they go along, laughing at each other's ideas.

Here's the premise: They cut comic-book "balloons"

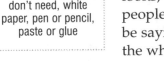

MATERIALS NEEDED:
Old photographs you don't need, white paper, pen or pencil, paste or glue

AGE OR SKILL LEVEL:
Able to write

out of blank white paper. (Or, as an alternative, they can cut out white strips of paper the width of the photographs.) In the balloons, they write what the people in the pictures might be saying or thinking. Or on the white strips, they write captions or titles or other funny addenda to the photos. Then they paste the balloons above or next to the speakers' heads, or the strips along the bottom of the photos.

Even dogs can talk or think in these pictures. . . . So what do you think Rover had in mind in that photo?

MIXED MEDIA ALPHABET BOOK

If your kids have a younger sibling, cousin, or neighbor who's of the age when alphabet books are appropriate, your kids can work together on producing a homemade but very serviceable alphabet book for that child.

They need fifteen sheets of construction paper: thirteen of them will have a letter of the alphabet on each side; the other two will be the covers of the book. Print the letters from A to Z on the pages, preferably both upper case and lower case. This can be done with crayon or paint. Then, whenever possible, they cut an appropriate picture from either an old photo that you don't need anymore, or from a magazine.

They'll need to look for pictures in which one thing can clearly be identified and cut out (arm, foot, hat, cat, house, television, xylophone), and in which that one item is not too tiny (nor too large) for the page. After they glue or paste the picture onto the page, they need to write the word on the page too. They may want to write it in all upper case letters, all lower case, or once each way.

At some point they'll want to give up on finding pictures for the troublesome pages—perhaps you don't subscribe to anything that has pictures of wildlife in it, and finding a zebra for the "Z" page seems hopeless. Or perhaps it's the "Q" or "X" that's the problem. At that point, before the kids throw their hands up in frustration and give up on the project, let them draw suitable pictures for those pages.

MATERIALS NEEDED:
Magazines, old photos, scissors, paste or glue, construction paper, crayons or paints

AGE OR SKILL LEVEL:
Able to write and spell

WHO AM I?

In the non-competitive version of this game, the object is simply for everyone to guess the name pinned on his back. Each person decides on a name of a person—living or dead, real or fictitious, famous or simply known to all the players—and writes it on a piece of paper, then pins it on the back of another person. As few as two people can play this, but the more the merrier.

In a two-person game, each person pins a name on the other person's back. In a three-person-or-more game, decide who will pin a name on whom. It doesn't really matter; there are no winners or losers, just a pair or group of kids out to have a good time guessing who they are supposed to be.

All questions must be answerable with a "yes" or "no":

"Am I male?"
"Am I alive?"
"Am I an adult?"

MATERIALS NEEDED:
Pieces of paper, pens or pencils, safety pins

AGE OR SKILL LEVEL:
Able to write

"Am I a real person?
"Am I a comic strip character?"
"Am I in a book?"
"Am I in a Disney movie?"
"Did I marry Cinderella?"
"Am I Prince Charming?"

Whether you will allow animals (Pluto, the Big Bad Wolf, Bugs Bunny, Lassie, Flicka) or stick strictly to people is a house rule that needs to be decided ahead of time. You can also narrow the scope of the game by playing Historical Who Am I?, Comic Strip Who Am I?, or any other delimiters you want to impose on the game.

Some of the questions inevitably become funny in the context of who the person to be guessed at is. The most innocent, natural questions take on a comic life in the light of who the guesser is supposed to be.

To prevent a cacophony of questions, it's best if you keep the questioning orderly, with each person asking a question in turn. It doesn't matter who asks first—there's no winner or loser, and nobody's supposed to be trying to be the first to guess her identity. It also doesn't matter whom a player asks— the person who pinned the note on her or another player.

Play continues till all the players have guessed their identities. (If a player gets stuck, there's no reason not to give him hints, since this is not a competition.)

TELEPHONE

The game of Telephone is great fun and utterly non-competitive. The winners in this game are the whole group, who all get to laugh at the unpredictable results. But the more people you have, the better, for this game. This is not a game for two or three people.

Get everyone into a circle, and decide who's going to start. The first person sets things in motion by *quickly* whispering a phrase or sentence into the ear of the person next to her. That person then whispers into the next person's ear what he thinks he heard from the first person. Player 3 now whispers into Player 4's ear what she thought she heard from Player 2. And so on.

When the phrase or sentence reaches the last person in the circle, he repeats aloud, for all to hear, what it was he thought he heard. Player 1 now says aloud what it was that she started passing around the circle. If Player 1 whispered, "George Washington wore wooden teeth," it's likely to come back to the final player as "George is washing but he wouldn't tease." Or "George's dome has wood in its tea." Rarely will a sentence make its way around the circle intact, and the more people there are, the more it's likely to get mangled.

MATERIALS NEEDED:
None

AGE OR SKILL LEVEL:
Four and up

BACK 'N' FORTH BOOKS

The premises this activity is built on are simple:

♦ Kids love to be read to.
♦ Kids who can read well love to read aloud and "show off."
♦ Kids love to emulate other kids.
♦ Reading is wonderful, and virtually anything that encourages kids to read is A Good Thing.

MATERIALS NEEDED:
Books

AGE OR SKILL LEVEL:
Able to read

Well then, let's all read. Get the best reader in your family, or among your child's friends, to start off by reading a page of a book, a short chapter in an easy "chapter book," or a page or two of a picture book. Then have him pass the book to another child.

How long a stretch of reading each child does will depend on the age and proficiency of the readers, their attention span, and the ease or difficulty of reading level of the book. But the basic premise is that one child reads to the others; then it's another's turn to read, with the book being passed along to each child.

If the book in question is a small picture book, and the readers are content to quit after one book, the activity will take up only a brief time. If, on the other hand, the book is a longer one, or the readers are gung-ho to keep going, the reading can stretch out over quite a long time, or can be a daily occurrence, with one or more chapters of a longer book being read aloud each day.

DO YOU SPEAK SPLABBLE?

Most kid-invented languages aren't really whole new languages complete with their own rules of grammar. What most of these are is a set of words that stand for words in English and are used in their place in an otherwise English sentence. For example: "Do you want to come to beglorron and fribble my clarn?" might be your son's way of asking his best friend, "Do you want to come to my house and read my comics?"

MATERIALS NEEDED:
Paper and pen or pencil

AGE OR SKILL LEVEL:
Seven and up

Kids can go as far as they want in inventing their own language. If they're young and not grammatically knowledgeable, or even if they're twelve years old but want to keep it simple, they can just think of words to replace key words in English, as above. If, on the other hand, they're older and fairly knowledgeable about grammar, they can get into the tricky business of verb forms, object versus subject pronouns, and as many other fine points as they care to deal with.

GUESS THE OUTCOME

Here's another pastime that will be of mild interest to the average child and fascinating to those who are really into statistics or math. The premise is simple: Think of questions surrounding the turning over of cards from a shuffled deck, then see what the answers are. For example:

MATERIALS NEEDED:
A deck of cards, possibly pen or pencil and paper

AGE OR SKILL LEVEL:
Seven and up

- How many times will you have to shuffle the deck and start a fresh deal before you turn over an ace on the first card?
- How many cards will it take before you turn over an ace after each of twenty shuffles?
- If you go through the entire deck, what is the greatest number of cards in a single suit to come up consecutively? Two hearts? Four diamonds?
- How many consecutively numbered cards (irrespective of suit) will you find in one time through a freshly shuffled deck?

- What's the longest string of alternating colors (red card, black card, red card, black card, etc.) you can turn over from a freshly shuffled deck before a wrongly colored card breaks the pattern?
- In one time through a freshly shuffled deck, can you turn up four cards in a row that follow alphabetical order (clubs, diamonds, hearts, spades)? If so, will it happen more than once?

DESIGN A CASTLE

Virtually every child, at some time, dreams of being a king or queen and living in a castle. The realities of living in a castle are something different from what kids imagine—just think of the heating problems, to begin with, and the walk from the bedchambers to the dining hall might require leaving for dinner fifteen minutes before it's scheduled to be served!—but there's no harm in dreaming.

If your kids really lived in a castle, what would their castle look

MATERIALS NEEDED:
Paper and pen or pencil

AGE OR SKILL LEVEL:
Eight and up

like? Why not give them a chance to design it? Though it's possible for two kids to cooperate on such a project and draw it together, you'll reduce the friction quotient if you suggest each child work on her own drawing. Will the castle have a moat? Turrets? How many rooms? Special features?

Even if their castle is only in the form of plans on paper, dreams are inexpensive—and fun.

AND ON THE EIGHTH DAY

Surely your kids have wondered, from time to time, what a dog would look like with an elephant's trunk, or what a *real* winged horse like Pegasus would look like, or what you would get if you could cross a tiger with a giraffe.

And if they're older, perhaps they've even heard of "lost species" or wondered whether dinosaurs are the only animals of long ago that are no longer around. They may be familiar with such mythical creatures as dragons and griffins, too, or with the tales of sea serpents that frightened Columbus's crew and other sailors of the time.

Here's a chance for their imaginations to run wild. Suppose they could cross any two real animals . . . what would they get? Suppose they were scientists digging in the ground, and they found a previously unknown and undiscovered species . . . what would it be? Suppose God had taken another day just to create more animals . . . what might he have fashioned on the eighth day? Suppose your kids could draw any animal they wanted, then wave a magic wand and have it come to life . . . what would they dream up? Whichever way you pose the question to them, they're bound to dream up—and draw or describe—some awfully fantastic creatures.

MATERIALS NEEDED:
Paper and pen or pencils or crayons

AGE OR SKILL LEVEL:
Six and up

TOP TEN LISTS

Top ten lists are a popular thing. You can probably credit (or blame) David Letterman, though he certainly didn't *invent* the things, he just made them a pervasive part of our culture.

Your kids, too, can compile top ten lists—whether funny or serious. For fun, they can do a list such as "Top ten excuses for not handing in homework," "Top ten reasons for failing a test," "Top ten excuses for staying up late," or "Top ten reasons I can't clean my room." On a more serious side, they can compile a "Top ten list of things we like about school" and "Top ten list of things we hate about school."

They can even compile a "Top ten annoying things parents do." Although, to be fair, they ought to then compile a "Top ten annoying things kids do to parents."

MATERIALS NEEDED:
Paper and pen or pencil

AGE OR SKILL LEVEL:
Eight and up

MY TOP TEN EXCUSES FOR NOT HANDING IN MY HOMEWORK

1. The dog ate it.
2. It blew away in the wind.
3. Martians came down from outerspace and needed to bring it back to their leader.
4. My Mom packed it away in her briefcase.
5. The baby threw up on it and I had to do it over again.
6. The power went out and it was too dark to finish.
7. A burglar broke in and stole it.
8. I left my workbook at school.
9. I was sick and couldn't do it.
10. I did it, but I did it in invisible ink so you can't see it.

CHAPTER TWO

BEANBAG
GAMES

W.C. Fields, in one of his movies, bragged that he'd competed at the Olympic level at Beanbag. "Many people were killed," he growled. Playing strictly noncompetitive beanbag games keeps the fatality count down to a reasonable level. Not only won't anyone get killed, very few fights should break out. (Far be it from me to promise zero fighting—where there are kids, there's going to be some fighting. It can even take place over a noncompetitive beanbag game. But it'll be down to a minimal level.)

There are any number of beanbags games that are or can be noncompetitive. One key in turning a normally competitive game into a noncompetitive version is to change the point or purpose of keeping score. If everyone's working for a common score, for instance, rather than for competitive individual scores, the game loses its cutthroat aspect. If Bradley's 20 points, Marcia's 22, and Chris's 19 are all added together, rather than compared against each other (with a resounding chorus of nyaah-nyaahs from the leader), the game becomes cooperative.

BUCKET BEANBAG

Instead of pitting contestant against contestant to see who can score the most baskets, the object of Bucket Beanbag, non-competitive style, dictates that everyone pool their scores to the common good. The goal to be aimed for is the eponymous bucket, or a wastebasket or other similar receptacle. This can be left standing on the floor or elevated on a chair, depending on both the heights and skill levels of the players. The distance from the bucket at which the players are to stand and toss their beanbags will have to be determined by a parent the first time—perhaps six feet away is a good distance for beginning players. Adjust that as needed for age and skill level.

You, the parent, will also have to set the goal score the first time: 25 tosses out of 100 need to score for the team to win, or 20 tosses out of 30. Choose goals that make sense given the age, skill, and attention spans of your kids. In subsequent games, they can set

MATERIALS NEEDED:
A bucket, wastebasket, or similar container; a reasonable quantity of beanbags—ten works well but is not essential; fewer can be used if necessary. For alternative games: More buckets/wastebaskets; a length of narrow board, a pole, or a broomstick; an empty soda can

AGE OR SKILL LEVEL:
Four and up if parents are scoring; otherwise, able to count to 100

their own goals. But the idea is that the kids are going to toss an aggregate total, among all players, and a certain number of those throws have to be baskets for the team to win.

The kids who really get into this activity in a big way may want to keep charts or graphs of their team's performances. They may eventually decide that their goal score isn't a set number but rather any number that is better than their last score: If last time they got 45 baskets out of 80 throws, this time, in order to win, they need to rack up 46 or better out of 80.

Off-Hand Bucket Beanbag
Play is the same as above, except that the players who are "righties" shoot with their left hand; "lefties" shoot with their right hand.

Comparative-Hand Bucket Beanbag
In this game, the object isn't to score a set number of points, but just to see how much better the team does shooting "usual-handedly" compared

with "off-handedly." The team shoots 100 (or some other number) times, with each player taking one shot at a time in rotation. Each player uses her usual hand. Then the team shoots the same number of times again, again in rotation with each player taking one shot at a time, this time with each player using her off-hand. Compare the difference in scores.

Bucket-Series Beanbag

Three buckets are set up in a row leading away from the players. Each player is given five beanbags and is to attempt to get at least one beanbag in each of the three buckets. If all the players succeed, the team wins.

To make the game harder and more interesting, set up more than three buckets and give each player a

larger number of beanbags, accordingly. (Of course you can also make the game harder by having the kids stand farther away from the target buckets, by elevating the buckets on chairs if you now have them on the floor, by requiring the kids to throw off-hand, or by giving each player only one extra beanbag, or no extras at all.)

Two-at-a-Time Bucket Beanbag

Each player holds two beanbags at a time, one in each hand. He tosses both at once, either at one bucket or at two buckets simultaneously, and attempts to score with both at once. If everyone on the team succeeds, the team wins. (Note: Though each player tosses his two beanbags simultaneously, the players are not all tossing at the same time; it is done in turn.)

If desired, rather than requiring that all the players succeed in order for the team to win, you can set a more easily attained goal: Say, each player gets four attempts to toss both beanbags at once and score. If the team succeeds in half its aggregate attempts, it is a winner.

Can-Can't

You've heard of the French dance, the can-can? Well this is the American game, the Can-Can't—the can can't fall or the point doesn't count. An empty soda can is set up on a board over the bucket, as above, and the players all aim for the bucket with their beanbags, but if they knock the can over, the point doesn't count.

Variation: If the can falls over, the team loses a point, regardless of whether a point was scored on that throw. In other words, if the team score stands at 45 baskets out of 75 throws, and Jeannie throws a beanbag and makes a basket but knocks over the can in the process, she wipes out her own point because she knocked over the can. The score now stands at 45 baskets out of 76 throws. The can is reset and James now throws a beanbag. He misses the bucket but still knocks over the can. The score now stands at 44 baskets out of 77 throws.

Lazy Bucket

The bucket is "lazy" because it's lying down on its side, and players need to throw their beanbags into the lying-down bucket . . . which isn't as easy as it may sound.

This game needs to be played in an open area where neither low-flying beanbags nor skidding buckets are likely to bang into Great-Aunt Maude's floor lamp, knocking it over.

BUCKET BEANBAG—"NFL" VERSION

The fantasies of sports fans know no limits, and if your kids like both beanbag games and professional sports, this game's a sure-fire winner. The object—again cooperative—is to have the players combine their efforts to give their favorite team the best possible season record.

How? Simple. Let's assume your kids are great fans of the Miami Dolphins. They write down a season's schedule—it doesn't have to be the real thing; it could even have the Dolphins pitted against the Russian Olympic Team one week and against Notre Dame the next. After all, this *is* a fantasy game!

Now they combine their beanbag-tossing talents to try to give the Dolphins an undefeated season. Jeff calls out the name of the opponent, and Gary, shooting his beanbag on behalf of the Dolphins, tries to beat Notre Dame. If he gets a basket, the Dolphins have won. Now he calls out the name of a team—the Russian Olympic Team is next on the schedule—and Jeff, shooting for the Dolphins, makes another basket.

MATERIALS NEEDED:
One beanbag, one bucket or wastebasket. For alternative versions: More beanbags, which for one alternative version need to be different colors

AGE OR SKILL LEVEL:
Six and up

Two-and-oh, the Dolphins have an undefeated season going for them. If the kids can get through the Dolphins' "schedule" without missing a basket, the team has had an undefeated season!

Of course, if your kids are fans of baseball, basketball, hockey, or soccer, they can be shooting on behalf of the Dodgers, the Bruins, or any other team. And if they follow college sports (perhaps because an older sister goes to Princeton or Eastern Illinois University), well then *that* can be the team they're shooting on behalf of.

Because getting the beanbag into the basket is a triumph for the players' favorite team, all successes and disappointments are associated with the team, rather than with the players. Of course if the Dolphins are playing a sixteen-game fantasy season and have won fifteen games so far, and then Jeff misses the basket with his beanbag on the final game of the season, he's likely to hear about it from his teammates. But still, that's not competition.

If the team has a winning season, they can go on to play in the Super

Bowl, or the Rose Bowl, or the World Series—whatever's appropriate.

Alternative version 1: It takes more than one beanbag to determine the outcome of a game. For instance, two averagely good players might toss three beanbags each, alternating turns. If four or more (which is more than half) of the total of six beanbags score into the bucket, the Dolphins have won. If only three (half the total thrown) go into the bucket, the game is a tie. And if two or fewer (less than half) of the beanbags make it into the bucket, the opponents—whoever that might be this week—have beaten the Dolphins. (Boooo!)

If the players don't like ties, an odd number of beanbags needs to be tossed, to avoid them. In a two-player game, players should alternate who is tossing the extra bag for the game.

Alternative version 2: Different-colored (or -sized, or -patterned) beanbags can be used, with some representing touchdowns and some representing field goals. For each game of the season, one player tosses twice, once for each team. (This is rather than one player tossing for the Dolphins, and one for the Rams, which could become a competitive game.) If Jerry tosses for both teams this time, John will toss for both teams next time.

After the players add up the total score—say, a field goal for each yellow beanbag that lands in the basket, and a touchdown for each calico beanbag that lands in the basket—they know that one team scored 10 points and the other scored six. But which team had the higher score?

One last beanbag has to be tossed. If it scores, your team had the winning score. If it misses, it was the opponents who racked up the greater number of points and won the game. (A coin toss can also be used to determine which team was victorious.)

BEANBAG SQUARES

The playing field for Beanbag Squares can be permanent—a marked-off section of the basement floor, perhaps—or it can be temporary. If you're setting up a fairly permanent field, use masking tape to delineate the required squares on a concrete, tile, or linoleum floor. If working with a temporary playing field, use a large piece of cardboard, marking it with tape, paint, or ink.

> **MATERIALS NEEDED:**
> Masking tape or a large piece of cardboard (perhaps 3 feet square) and paint or ink; beanbags

> **AGE OR SKILL LEVEL:**
> Four and up

The ten squares that comprise the playing field should be about one foot in length on each side. The configuration in which you set them up is optional: You can put them in a triangular pattern like that of ten bowling pins, in two rows of five squares each, or in some random pattern. The squares can all be touching or totally separated.

One house rule you need to work out in advance is how to score a beanbag that lands so it's straddling two (or more) squares. You have three options:

♦ Only beanbags that land fully in one square count for score. If any part of the beanbag is lying outside the lines of a square, it doesn't score.

♦ The beanbag garners the score written in the highest-yielding box of those it's touching.

♦ The beanbag earns a score equal to the total of the scores written in all the boxes it's touching. Conceivably (though it's highly unlikely), if you have all your boxes touching each other, a beanbag could land right on four corners and be partially in each of four squares, earning the total of the scores for all of the four.

Now what about those scores—how are you to number the boxes, anyhow? Conventionally, they are numbered from 1 to 10, with the boxes farthest away having the higher scores. But there is no real requirement for this numbering scheme, and you can feel free to use any other method that suits you.

The lag line behind which players stand and toss from should be a reasonable distance from the boxes. What constitutes "reasonable" is going to depend on the strength and skill of the players. Making a beanbag come to rest in a particular square should be a challenging task yet not an impossible one. I'd suggest you have your kids toss a few beanbags at the target boxes from varying distances, see how well they fare, then establish the location of the lag line accordingly.

Now what are the various games that fall within the overall classification of "Beanbag Squares"?

Beanbag Birthday

The object here is for the players to celebrate all of their birthdays by tossing beanbags onto the appropriate "dates" on the playing field. Since you probably don't have a square marked "11" for those born in November, and you surely don't have a square marked "86" for those born in that year, how are you going to work it?

Easy! Throw for each numeral separately. If Amy's birthday is June 22, 1986, or 6/22/86, Amy's goal is to throw beanbags into the squares marked "6," "2," "2" (again), "8," and "6" (again). When she has accomplished this—in however many turns it takes her—it is Jennifer's turn. (Note that if Amy gets an 8 before she has gotten the first 6 and the two 2s, it doesn't count; the boxes have to be achieved in the correct order.)

When all the kids on the team have achieved scoring into their birthday numbers, the team has won. It stands to reason that a child who was born on 2/3/82 has fewer squares to toss into than a child who was born

on 10/24/83, but as the kids are not competing on this one, the perceived inequity has no real validity. The child who has six squares to toss for instead of four has the advantage of more fun and the disadvantage of more frustration (and those two probably balance each other out), but since she is not competing against the other player(s), there's no unfair advantage or disadvantage.

Progression

Players cooperate in trying to land beanbags in the boxes 1 through 10, in order. Only after getting into the "1" square is the "2" square aimed for, and so forth.

This can be accomplished in either of two ways:

1. Each player throws at the boxes from "1" to "10" in order, landing in all ten boxes before the next player takes his turn. Since this is not a competition, there is no reason to keep track of how many turns it takes each player to succeed. The game is simply over when everyone has succeeded.
2. The players rotate turns. Liz throws into the "1" square. Tony now aims for the "2" square. Next it's Roger's turn; if Tony succeeded in hitting the "2" square, Roger aims for "3." If Tony missed, Roger aims for "2." Now it's Lucia's turn. Assuming Roger landed a beanbag in "2," Lucia is shooting for "3." If he missed, she's still shooting for "2."

The game is over when all ten squares have been landed in in order.

Variation for particularly skilled players: The numbers not only must be earned in order but also *without hitting any numbers out of order*. That is, after Joan lands her beanbag in "1," the next throw *must* be into "2." If it lands anywhere else she's got to start over with "1." She might be up to "9," but if her last throw lands in anything but "10," she has to start all over again at "1."

Each player completes throwing into "1" through "10" in order, as above, before the next player takes her turn.

Score 100

In this game, players work together to score 100 points. Tossing alternately, the players keep the running total of their combined points.

In the more difficult version of the game, it is necessary for the point total to reach exactly 100. If the score total thus far is 97 and the beanbag lands in the "8" square, the toss doesn't count. The players must continue tossing till they either land the beanbag in the "3" square or, at least, land it in the "1" or "2" squares, at which point they need either a "2" or "1" to reach 100.

In the easier version, it is only necessary to reach *or exceed* 100, so that scoring into the "7" square with a total of 96 would be perfectly acceptable, even though it gives a total of 103, three points over the required total. Any toss that brings the total into three figures would be considered a success in the cooperative quest for 100.

Addition

In this game, principally for younger kids, two players each toss a beanbag onto the playing field. The numbers of the two squares the beanbags landed in are written on paper in the form of an ordinary addition problem.

Play continues for a previously agreed-upon number of rounds. When ten (let's say) pairs of numbers have been written down, the players do the addition in all ten problems, after which they add up all ten sums for their total score.

Sneaky, how we parents make them practice math when they just want to play, isn't it?

SpellBag

For this game, you'll need letters as well as numbers in the ten squares. Write the letters of the alphabet in the ten squares in order (using tape, paint, or ink), returning to the "1" square to continue the alphabet after you reach the "J" in the "10" square. The "1" square will also have "A" and "K" and "U" written in it; the "2" square has "B" and "L" and "V"; the "3" square has "C" and "M" and "W." (The "7" through "10" squares will only have two letters in them; the "1" through "6" squares will have three letters in them.)

Now that each box on the playing field has letters as well as numbers in it, games similar to some of those explained above, but involving letters instead of numbers, can be played. For instance, instead of tossing for their birthdates, players can spell their names. Instead of cycling through the numbers 1 through 10, players can cycle through the alphabet. Players can even attempt to spell entire sentences, perhaps sending messages to each other, each player spelling out her reply to the preceding sentence.

When spelling a word, a single toss can be counted for only one letter at a time. A boy named Karl, trying to spell his name, who lands the beanbag in the "1" square has landed it in the square for both "A" and "K," but the toss counts only for the "K" the first time; he must toss into the same square again to rack up the "A" he needs to keep spelling his name.

Spelling games can be beneficial in four ways. First, the kids are learning to play cooperatively. Second, they are involved in physical activity that requires and gives practice in coordination. Third, they are practicing spelling. And fourth, if they are required to spell something other than CAT, DOG, or their names, they can learn some additional information—for instance, if they are spelling the names of the planets, they will learn the names of all of them.

The possibilities for beanbag spelling are limited only by the number of words in the language. That ought to keep them busy for at least a part of an afternoon!

BEANBAG TOSS

This is fun for as few as two to as many as twenty kids.

With two kids, have them stand almost nose to nose. One child throws the beanbag, and the other catches it. Now the child holding the beanbag takes one tiny step backward before throwing it again. After the other child catches the beanbag, he now takes one tiny step backward. The kids keep taking one tiny step away with each catch, the object being to keep from missing the beanbag while the gap between the two is ever wider.

When one child does finally miss, the two get back together and begin throwing the beanbag again, repeating the process, seeing if they can get even farther apart this time before someone drops the beanbag. The game continues till they tire of it.

With three kids playing, they form a sort of triangle, tossing the beanbag from Player 1 to Player 2 to Player 3, each one taking a tiny step back after catching the beanbag.

With four or more kids playing, you have two options:

MATERIALS NEEDED:
One beanbag

AGE OR SKILL LEVEL:
Three and up

Option # 1: Everyone gets in a circle, with the beanbag being tossed around the circle. Periodically everyone takes one tiny step back.

Option # 2: Everyone forms two straight lines facing each other. The first player tosses the beanbag to the child across from her, who tosses it to the child next to the child who started, who in turn tosses it to the child next to the first catcher, and so on down the line, if there are more than four kids playing.

After everyone has had the beanbag, the last to catch it holds it while everyone takes one tiny step backward, and then play starts all over again with the beanbag being tossed back up the line in the direction it came from. When it reaches the last child, everyone takes a tiny step back and the beanbag is tossed back down the line again.

Keep going till someone drops it. Then start over, with everyone very close together again. Continue till the kids grow bored and want to play something else.

CHAPTER THREE

OTHER ACTIVE GAMES

CHAIRS APLENTY

In this variation on musical chairs, there are more chairs than there are kids, and nobody gets left without a seat. But the music changes tempo quickly, so the kids need to be alert.

It's best if you can supply the music yourself, either with a piano, a guitar, or some other instrument. If you're not musically inclined, however, you can put together a tape with a minute or so of fast music, a minute of slow music, a minute of placid music, a minute of a march, and so on. Make sure to stop the music here and there throughout the tape, not necessarily between tempos, but sometimes right in the middle of a passage of music.

It's necessary to spend some time in advance putting the tape together, but the effort will pay off in the fun the

MATERIALS NEEDED:
More chairs than there are kids playing, source of music (cassette recorder, or piano, guitar, or other instrument)

AGE OR SKILL LEVEL:
Three and up

kids have, and the tape is usable over and over.

Whenever the music stops, the kids have to sit down, and whenever it starts up again, the kids have to resume circling the line of chairs in time to the music. You can stop playing in the middle of an Irish jig, resume playing the jig, slow down to a funereal number, speed it up to a march, stop playing, resume the march, and so on. The kids will scramble to keep up. And everyone has a good time. And since there are chairs aplenty and no competition, nobody gets left out, nobody loses, and a good time is had by all.

MUSICAL PILE-UP

Here's another variation on Musical Chairs. In this version, as with Musical Chairs, when you start playing music the participants walk around the chairs, which are alternately facing front and back. And, as with Musical Chairs, when you stop the music, each participant sits quickly into a chair if he can, there not being enough chairs for all the participants. But unlike Musical Chairs, no one is out. If there isn't a chair for a particular player, he just falls into someone else's lap.

Since you have provided several fewer chairs than there are players (say, two chairs for three or four players, three or four chairs for six players), some players will have one

MATERIALS NEEDED:
A few fewer chairs than there are players, source of music

AGE OR SKILL LEVEL:
Three and up

or more other players in their laps. You may wind up with three kids sitting on three other kids' laps, or even two or three kids piling onto one lap.

There is no formal end to the game—it's over when everyone's had enough.

This is not a decorous game, but it isn't competitive. The kids may be boisterous as they scramble to get to the chairs, and they may plop onto laps a little harder than they need to, but nobody's left out, nobody loses, and everybody has fun.

JELLY SEEK

The larger the house you live in, the more possibilities for this game, but even if you live in a two-bedroom apartment, and if we eliminate the bathrooms as a hiding place, you've got at minimum two bedrooms, a kitchen, a living room, and possibly a dining room or a hallway in which your kids can hide jelly-beans from each other.

MATERIALS NEEDED:
One jellybean for each room of the house

AGE OR SKILL LEVEL:
Three and up

Divide the rooms of the house equally between the kids: Jeri gets your bedroom and the living room; Roberta gets the room she shares with Jeri and the kitchen. Or, in a larger house and with more kids, Ryan gets all three bedrooms, Rob gets the living room, kitchen, and foyer, and Rich gets the dining room, laundry room, and family room.

Each child now hides one jellybean in each room. When all are hidden, the kids trade rooms (if there are more than two kids playing, agree on who's searching which rooms), and everyone hunts for the jellybeans.

Notes:

♦ You may want to establish ground rules in advance: No opening your sister's dresser drawers; keep out of Dad's closet; keep out of the knife drawer in the kitchen; or whatever other house rules seem called for.

♦ If the kids opt to, they can provide coded clues, obscure treasure maps, or other guides to the secreted goodies, guides that may be more baffling than the game itself.

Variations:

♦ Instead of hiding one jellybean in each room, hide two, or three—but it must be agreed in advance what the number is, and each child must stick to it consistently.

♦ One room of each child's three (or more—this doesn't work as well if each child is only assigned two)

rooms is to be passed by—but the kids are not to tell which room they did *not* hide a jellybean in. So if Maura hid jellybeans in two of three rooms, Jeff does not know which of the three rooms he is searching through in vain.

♦ Instead of all the kids searching simultaneously, all the kids can band together as each child seeks the jellybeans. Maura can have great fun watching Jeff walk right past her super secret hiding place ten times and never think to look under Mom's jewelry tray. Jeff can really get a kick out of Maura's frustration as she turns the living room upside down and never finds the jellybean under the throw rug under the coffee table.

SHEETBALL

Sheetball is the game of throwing a ball through a hole in a suspended sheet from a reasonable distance.

Start by deciding how you're going to hang the sheet. If you have a clothesline in your back yard, that's your best bet. If not, you need to find another means of suspending the sheet. You could hang it over a low tree limb if there are no branches to interfere. What other possibilities are available in your yard I leave for you to discover.

If you drape the sheet in half over a clothesline or a tree limb, you'll need to cut two holes, one each in the front and back halves of the sheet. If you hang the sheet with clothespins and there's only one thickness of sheet hanging, you of course only need to cut one hole.

How large should the hole be? This depends on the size of the ball and the ages of the players. Two six-year-olds will need a bigger hole than a pair or trio of eleven-year-olds. (Or else they'll need to stand closer, or both.) Kids playing with a basketball will need a larger hole than kids playing with a pink rubber ball or tennis ball, or an old, "dead" ping-pong ball. (Golf balls, with their hardness and ability to hurt someone or break a window, are not recommended.)

MATERIALS NEEDED:
Ball, old sheet you don't mind cutting up, scissors, clothesline or other arrangement for hanging sheet

AGE OR SKILL LEVEL:
Able to throw a ball at least three feet with some accuracy

How close should the kids stand to the sheet? Let them try throwing from different distances; when they find one that's moderately hard, challenging but not frustrating, they've found the right place to stand. And again, there's no contest here, no winners, so it's better for them to stand far enough away to make it reasonably difficult to score. If it's too easy, it won't be as much fun.

As the kids get better at scoring through the hole in the sheet, they can practice trick shots: with their eyes closed; throwing under one raised leg; standing backward and throwing over the head; throwing with the "other" hand (left for a righty; right for a lefty); twirling around three times quickly and then throwing fast; and any other tricks they can think of.

SCRAMBLED NONRACE

A perennial favorite at field days and school and church picnics, the egg race in its original form involves players racing from Point A to Point B carrying an egg on a spoon. If they race so fast that they drop and break the egg, they're out.

The non-competitive form of this activity involves two or more players walking as briskly as they're comfortable doing, abreast of each other, while each holds an uncooked egg, in its shell, on a teaspoon. The players do not race. They do not attempt to get to where they're going faster than each other. They *do* attempt to arrive with their eggs intact.

> **MATERIALS NEEDED:**
> One teaspoon and one uncooked egg in its shell for each player

> **AGE OR SKILL LEVEL:**
> Four and up

Where they're going will depend on where they're playing. If you live in the city on a busy street, and have no backyard, better wait till your next visit to the park before you engage in a Scrambled Nonrace. If you have a big back yard, your goal can be the oak tree by the back fence and back to the screen door.

Remember, it's not a race. If someone does get to the goal point ahead of the others, that doesn't make him or her a winner. And if someone drops an egg (as is probable), that doesn't make him or her a loser.

But it may make him or her kind of wet and yucky!

PARTNERSHIP BOWLING

The usual thing when two kids go bowling is for them to compete to see who can get the best score. This is natural and logical. It can also lead to fights and arguments. And when one child is much older or more proficient than the other, it can be downright unsatisfactory.

A good alternative is to have them bowl in partnership rather than in competition. For the first game, let Josh roll the first ball of every frame and Seth bowl "clean-up," rolling the second ball and trying to make a spare. Then play another game and reverse the positions, with Seth bowling first and Josh trying to capitalize on the pins he's knocked down by getting as many of the rest as he can.

MATERIALS NEEDED:
Your friendly neighborhood bowling alley

AGE OR SKILL LEVEL:
Some bowling ability

This arrangement emphasizes teamwork rather than competition while still preserving the basic goal of bowling: to knock down the most pins possible for the highest score.

BLOB TAG

In Blob Tag, It starts out as one person, in the time honored manner, but as each player gets tagged, she becomes part of It, and all the different players who make up It have to remain attached by holding on to each other—either holding hands, or holding on to each other's clothing.

The game is best played with a relatively large number of players—at least five. The game starts out like any ordinary game of Tag, with one player chosen as It and all the other players scurrying away from him. But when It tags the first player—let's say it's Jeremy—Jeremy becomes part of It.

Holding on to the original It's hand, arm, or clothing, Jeremy joins the original It as they chase after the next nearest player— we'll say that's Maureen. When they tag Maureen she becomes part of It, holding

MATERIALS NEEDED:
None

AGE OR SKILL LEVEL:
Four and up

the hand, arm, or clothing of either the original It or Jeremy, and staying with them as they rove the playing field at a brisk pace, trying to tag someone else.

It doesn't matter which part of It tags a player, the original It or one of the subsequent additions.

The fun in this game is in the running and laughing, rather than in any attempt to win. The fun is also in the ludicrous experience of having several linked-together kids try to run in a coordinated and cooperative way in pursuit of the others, across and around and all over a backyard (or other playing field), without bumping into each other or falling as they change course and keep running.

Tag! You're part of It!

THREE DEEP

Three Deep is a chase game for a large group (fourteen or more if possible), but one with no winners or losers, just fun. Instead of an It, there is a Pursuer and a Pursued, but typically no one remains in either role very long.

Choose a player to start as the Pursuer, and another as the Pursued. All the other players form two circles, with one circle inside the other. There should be about a foot of space between the two circles, and about three or more feet of space between players in the outer circle. All players in both circles face the center.

The Pursuer now begins chasing the Pursued around the outside of the circle. At some point, the Pursued breaks into the middle of the circle and stands in front of the player she finds herself nearest to. This means that at one point the players are Three Deep.

Since a Three Deep configuration is not permissible, the player in the inner circle whom the former Pursued has stood in front of now moves backward, and the player behind him, in the outer circle, who has been displaced is now forced to become the Pursued. Breaking away from her former spot, she starts running around the circle, trying to elude the Pursuer. But of course, any time she wants, she can evade the Pursuer by running into the circle, forming a Three Deep, causing two players to step backward and the rearmost of them to become the new Pursued.

If at any point a Pursuer tags a Pursued, they trade places, the former Pursued now becoming the Pursuer and vice versa.

Pursuit does not take place inside the circle. As soon as the Pursued runs into the circle, the Pursuer stops chasing her and prepares to chase the new Pursued.

Just as there is no winner or loser in this game, there is no formalized end to it, either. It's simply over when everyone's had enough.

MATERIALS NEEDED:
None

AGE OR SKILL LEVEL:
Five and up

STATUES

Only a mildly competitive game to begin with, Statues can be played completely non-competitively if you remove the selection of the best statue by It at the end of the game. It's a good game for a large group, though small groups can play too, and is better played outdoors than indoors so players can spin around without worrying about smashing into furniture.

MATERIALS NEEDED:
None

AGE OR SKILL LEVEL:
Four and up

Statues is another of those rare games in which it's an honor to be It; the first thing players need to do is decide who's going to be It for the first game. This is probably best accomplished with the fewest squabbles by using a traditional counting-out rhyme such as "One Potato" or another of that ilk, though any other means, such as selecting the

youngest or oldest to be It first is equally acceptable.

The job of It is to spin the other players around. It takes each of the other players, one by one, by one hand. That player holds his hand out, and It spins him around in a circle. At last It releases the other player, who goes staggering across the open space they're playing in, off-balance from the spinning, till It yells "Freeze!" or "Statues!" (the different calls are regional). At that time, the player is required to hold perfectly still, no matter what grotesque position he's in, and hold the pose.

He probably is in a ridiculous position to begin with, and maintaining that position—which may involve one arm up in the air, one foot off the ground, and the mouth twisted in a silly grin— is even funnier (and difficult!). This provides much of the merriment of the game . . . but wait, you other players who are laughing . . . you're going to be silly statues too!

One by one, It spins each player, till all are frozen statues in bizarre positions.

In the mildly competitive original form of the game, It would now choose the best statue of the lot, and that player would become It for the next game. But as this is the non-competitive version, everyone should just peek at the other statues as well as they can without changing position, laugh at the sillier examples, then regroup and choose a new It by whatever method they used before.

If the youngest was chosen to be the first It, the second-youngest would now become It; if the oldest, then the second-oldest becomes It. If a counting-out method was used, all players *except the one who was It already* should again use the same rhyme or other method to determine the next It.

If possible, everyone should have a turn at being It, unless the group is large and time is limited, or the players are getting tired of the game and want to move on to some other game.

DUCK DUCK GOOSE

Depending on your viewpoint, this game is either totally non-competitive or only very mildly competitive. There's an It, and a lot of chasing, but no winner or loser, and no formal end to the game.

Choose someone to be the first It. All the other players squat in a circle, while It walks around the outside of the circle, behind the players, tapping each child on the shoulder as she passes. Each time It taps a player on the shoulder, she says, "Duck." She continues around the circle, tapping players and saying, "Duck. Duck. Duck. Duck," till finally, tapping one child, she says "Goose."

The child so designated jumps up and runs around the circle. It runs too. Both scramble to get around the circle and back to the space vacated by the player It designated as "Goose." If It gets there first, she takes the space and the other player becomes the new It. If the other player returns to his former space first, he takes the space again, and It remains as It.

MATERIALS NEEDED:
None

AGE OR SKILL LEVEL:
Three and up

In a large group, the "Goose" has a fair chance of pulling ahead of It and getting back to the space first. As a practical matter, though, It has a head start and in most small groups will get back to the space first, virtually ensuring a new It for each round.

The game simply is over when enough of the kids are tired of playing it that they agree to play something else.

GO IN AND OUT THE WINDOW

Here's an old standard that kids have been playing for generations, possibly centuries. You probably played it yourself as a child, but if you don't remember the tune, make one up or "sing-song" the words. It's good for a mid- to large-sized group of young kids and is a gentle game, with no winner, no loser, and no real purpose other than having fun and moving to music. There is an It, but in this game being It is an honor, not a punishment.

The players form one large circle with ample space between each of the players, as It is going to be weaving in and out of the circle, around the other players. As the players sing, It walks in front of one player, behind the next, in front of the next, behind the next, and so on. When the song is over, It kneels in front of the player she finds herself in front of, kneels down, and bows her head. This player now becomes It, trading places with the former It and weaving in and out of the circle as play starts over.

I have heard various versions of the verses. The first one seems to be pretty generally rendered as:

Go in and out the window,
Go in and out the window,
Go in and out the window,
As we have done before.

Other verses I have heard in different versions include:

Now stand and face your partner,
Now stand and face your partner,
Now stand and face your partner,
As we have done before.

Now follow me to London,
Now follow me to London,
Now follow me to London,
As we have done before.

MATERIALS NEEDED:
None

AGE OR SKILL LEVEL:
Three and up

THE FOX AND THE COLORED EGGS

At least four players are needed for this game. One plays the fox, one plays the grocer, and the other two (or more) play eggs. The eggs each decide what color they will be, and each whispers his color in the grocer's ear quietly enough that the fox doesn't hear them. They need to pick different colors from each other, and if two (or more) have picked the same color, the grocer needs to tell the second (third, etc.) player to pick a different color.

The fox then walks up to the grocer, while the eggs crouch nearby. The grocer says, "Good morning, Mr. Fox. What can I help you with today?"

The fox answers, "I would like to buy some eggs."

The grocer asks, "What color eggs would you like?"

The fox replies with a color—let's say orange.

MATERIALS NEEDED:
No materials, but a reasonable amount of space to run in

AGE OR SKILL LEVEL:
Four and up

If none of the "eggs" has chosen orange for his color, the grocer says, "I'm sorry, Mr. Fox, but we're fresh out of orange eggs today." The fox keeps asking for a color, and the grocer keeps replying the same way.

But eventually— whether on the first try or the fifth or whatever—the fox is going to guess a color that was chosen by one of the eggs. At that point, the player who chose that color jumps up and runs to the edge of the playing area, with the fox running after him.

The game is over. Now the players who were the fox and the grocer become eggs, and the players who were the eggs—or two of them, if there were more than two—become the fox and the grocer. The eggs choose new colors, and the game starts all over again.

THE OGRE IN THE ATTIC

This simple game for the really small set requires at least three players. One is the mommy, one is the ogre, and the other player is the child. If there are four or more players, anyone who isn't the mommy or the ogre is a child. As I describe the game, below, I'll refer to one mommy, one ogre, and one child, but keep in mind that although there is always just one mommy and one ogre, there can be as many children as you want.

The ogre crouches off to the side, or behind a big bush or tree (if playing outdoors), or a big piece of furniture (if playing indoors). The mommy tells the child something like, "I have to go out in the garden now, and I'm leaving you alone in the house for just three minutes. Can you behave yourself that long? If you do, you'll get a treat."

The mommy walks away and the child is left by herself. She plays for a couple of minutes; then the mommy returns and says, "For being so good, you may have a treat. Go up into the attic and see what I have hidden in the old suitcase."

Going up "into the attic" (in the direction where the ogre is crouching or hiding), the child goes slowly, getting ever nearer the lurking, "hidden" ogre. At an appropriate moment, the ogre pounces, making a scary noise and chasing the child.

The game is over, and it's time to play again, with everyone changing roles. If there are two or more players playing children, one or more will have to be children again, but play it again and again and eventually everyone will get a turn at being the mommy and the ogre.

MATERIALS NEEDED:
None, although it's nice if the kids can play this where there is a chair, bush, or other large object for the ogre to hide behind. This is not necessary, though.

AGE OR SKILL LEVEL:
Three and up

HOOP-DE-DOO

If your house is like many others across America, it has more than one hoop lying around. That is, besides the basketball hoop that probably graces your garage, you quite probably have a hula hoop or two lying around in your attic or garage.

Have I got ways for your kids to use them!

Of course your kids can use them in the manner for which they were originally invented—giving their hips the ol' Elvis rotation to keep a hoop aloft around the waist. But I have other suggestions beyond that, ideas for ways the kids can use one or more hula hoops to play non-competitive games.

MATERIALS NEEDED:
Hula hoops

AGE OR SKILL LEVEL:
Five and up

Catch

Two kids stand ten to twenty feet apart and roll the hoops back and forth at each other. There's a quantity of skill involved in getting the hoop to roll, and to get it to go in the direction you want. Your kids should quickly pick up the ability to guide the hoop with some accuracy—and they'll likely laugh their heads off during the learning process.

Certain wrist motions will cause the hoop to "boomerang"—to stop in its tracks and roll back at you (see "Rollback"), so experimenting with how to roll the hoop may result in some funny and unintentional results. But if the kids persevere, they'll get the hang of it. But experimenting with how to propel a plastic ring across the grass is part of the fun, and eventually the actual "catch" can proceed.

Let the games begin!

Double Catch

If your kids have access to two hoops, a twist can be added to the basic game of Catch. Instead of rolling a single hoop back and forth from Jeannie to Tom, the kids each have a hoop and roll them to one another simultaneously.

As Tom catches the hoop Jeannie just sent spinning across the lawn, she catches the one he just propelled. Then they each send back the hoops they just caught. Ideally, they aim for controlling the spin and speed so that each catches at the same time, rethrows immediately, and catches again in sync with the other player.

If things are working as they should, the two hoops will pass each other at the midpoint of the lawn. On some occasions, however, an extra wobble in the spin, or a hoop hitting a stone or an ant mound will throw one hoop slightly off course and cause it to veer into the other hoop. As the hoops collide, the kids will laugh—and set off to retrieve them so the game can continue.

Collision

As in Double Catch, above, the players stand ten to twenty feet apart and roll the two hoops toward each other. But, unlike Double Catch, where collisions are a funny but unwanted occurrence, here the aim is to deliberately cause the two hoops to collide.

Variation: In this version of collision, sometimes called Trap Shoot, one player rolls his hoop across the lawn in front of the other player, rather than aiming at her. The second player rolls her hoop at a time that she thinks will cause it to intercept the first hoop, collide with it, and knock it down.

If you haven't gotten a good mental picture of what I'm talking about, picture a clock face with the two players standing at 6 and 9. Player 9 rolls her hoop straight across the clock face toward 3. Player 6

sends his hoop out toward 12, trying to hit the first hoop as it crosses the place in the center of the clock face where the hands are attached.

Far from a competition, this activity requires concentrated cooperation, teamwork in trying to get the two hoops to collide at the midpoint. Players take turns as to who rolls first and who intercepts.

Rollback

If you toss a hoop out in front of you with a flick of your wrist that imparts backspin to the hoop, an interesting thing happens. When the hoop hits the ground in a position to roll, instead of continuing its away-from-you motion, the backspin will cause it to head back toward you. (Note that a person can play catch with himself with a hula hoop by using the backspin to cause the hoop to roll back to the thrower.)

In two-player Rollback, the kids stand alongside each other, a few feet apart, from which position each throws her hoop. As the hoops hit the lawn and begin rolling back toward the players, the kids quickly switch places. The object of the game is to catch the hoop that the other player threw.

Requiring no great dexterity or skill beyond mastering the motion to create a backspin, it's a simple pastime, but it's simply fun.

Through the Hoop

Players stand in the same positions relative to each other as they did for Trapshoot, but only one hoop is used. The first player rolls the hoop across the grass. The second player then attempts to jump through the rolling hoop without knocking it down.

Some skill is involved here. Gauging the trajectory and speed of the rolling hoop takes some experience, and projecting your own body to keep it from coming into contact with the hoop is a good physical enterprise. The satisfaction of tumbling onto the grass and watching the hoop you've just jumped through rolling merrily on its way gives great satisfaction.

The rolling hoop can also be propelled with a backspin—requiring greater dexterity and a greater ability to judge distance and trajectory.

Players can take turns being the roller and the jumper.

Ring Toss

One player stands still, playing the part of a peg, while the other player tosses the hoop(s) at him, trying to score a ringer by making the hoop drop over the "peg" player. The person who is playing the peg may want to cover his face with his hands, to protect against the unskilled throw that might propel the edge of the hoop against the—ouch!—bridge of the nose.

Jump Rope

A hoop can be used as a peculiar kind of jump rope. Learning the skills required to get the hoop into a steady jump rope motion is a relatively easy matter. Two hands are required to hold the hoop for jumping, at something like the eleven o'clock and one o'clock positions on the hoop—your kids can experiment to see what's the best position for them.

The kids can simply jump for the fun of it, or they can set a goal, such as two kids, each with a hoop, trying to get up to 100 without either of them missing.

Hoopscotch

If you have more than just a couple of hoops in your attic, or you know of friends and neighbors with hoops tucked away that you may borrow, there are a few more games your kids can play.

Hoops can be laid out on the lawn in whatever pattern seems attractive to the players. They can be placed in a single line, or laid out in two parallel lines, similar to the shape of a hopscotch court, or they can be laid out in a totally random arrangement.

I'm assuming a fairly large number of hoops for this activity—about eight. If these games turn out to be popular with your kids, Hoopscotch rings can be rigged out of lengths of rope, garden hose, or other makeshift objects that give you a circle on the lawn.

There aren't specific rules for Hoopscotch. The idea is simply to interact in creative ways with the circles lying there in the yard. All the kids can progress from hoop to hoop by various means of locomotion, either jumping or hopping on two feet (bunny-hopping), hopping on one foot, alternately hopping on one foot, then two, then one, and so on, hopping backward, or whatever other motions they can think of. Your kids can make up lots of silly and/or difficult maneuvers that they can have a good time fooling around with.

VOLLEY UP

Though an actual game of ping-pong, badminton, or tennis can be highly competitive, merely taking racquet in hand does not predetermine the playing of a competitive game. Not only can volleying be non-competitive, it's good practice for a real game at another time.

The object is to see how long you can keep the ball or shuttlecock in play. The two (or four) players volley back and forth, making a supreme effort to serve playable shots right to each other. With each hit, the players count loudly and proudly, "One - two - three - four," and onward as high as they can get before someone misses.

The "score" is the result of a team effort, an effort to keep the game going, and any competition is simply for the players to beat their own previous high score and keep the ball or shuttlecock in motion even longer this time.

MATERIALS NEEDED:
Ping-pong ball, paddles, and table; or badminton net, racquets, and shuttlecock; or tennis ball, rackets, and court

AGE OR SKILL LEVEL:
Some ability at either ping pong, tennis, or badminton

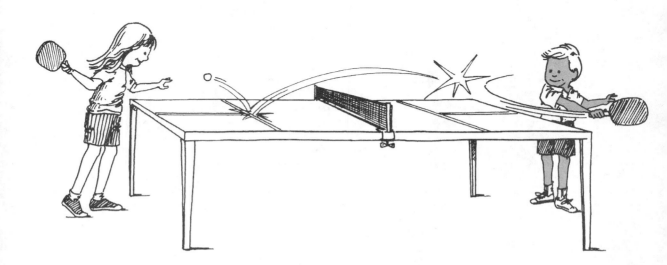

WALK 'N' ROLL

Talk about pointless! Talk about goofy! Talk about fun! Playable indoors or out, this game is better in an area where there's plenty of room to walk around but can also be managed in more cramped quarters.

MATERIALS NEEDED:
One die (or a pair of dice for Variation 3)

AGE OR SKILL LEVEL:
Six and up

Two throws of the die will determine how many steps the players are to take and in which direction. The first player stands approximately in the middle of the area, throws the die, announces the count, and then repeats the process for a second throw.

The first throw of the die determines the motion. Here's what the rolls mean:

1: Move straight ahead.
2: Make a quarter-turn to your right and move in that direction.
3: Turn 180 degrees (face the opposite direction from your starting position) and move in that direction.
4: Make a quarter-turn to your left and move in that direction.
5: Walk straight backward.
6: Run around in a tight circle, returning to your starting point.

The second throw of the die determines the number of steps you take in each direction—unless you rolled a 6 the first time. A 6 doesn't call for a second roll of the die, as the size of the move is predetermined.

Now that you understand the basic rules of movement in the game, let's look at the different versions of playing it:

Version 1: Each player rolls for the other, the walker moving once the second roll has told her how far to go, then immediately rolling for the other player.

Version 2: One player walks all the time, with the other player rolling steadily and calling out the directions and the distances: "Forward, three," "To your right, two," "Straight backward, six," "Turn halfway, one," "Straight backward, four," "Turn in a tight circle." This will keep the walker fairly constantly in motion, turning in various directions and lurching this way and that, rather like the proverbial drunken sailor.

Version 3: This calls for a pair of dice, one die for each player to hold in his hand. (Theoretically more than two could play in a large enough area, in which case more dice would be needed.) In this version, players move at the same time. They should close their hands around their dice tightly enough to keep the dice from falling but loosely enough to roll them around. When the roll is stopped, the hand is opened, and the die is left lying on the palm. Whatever number is up is the number that will determine the direction; repeat to determine number of steps. Players move almost continually.

ROCK AROUND THE BLOCK

For generations, kids have found fascination in kicking stones, crumpled-up soda cans, and other small, lightweight, kickable objects in front of them as they walked down the street. For just as many generations, parents have decried the practice as deleterious to shoe leather.

But in today's world, where most kids wear sneakers rather than leather shoes, the only harm in indulging in the practice would come from kicking something painfully heavy or sharp, from following it into a busy street if it went off course, or from kicking it into the shins of a passing pedestrian.

Today's kids aren't much into walking, which is unfortunate, given that it's one of the best forms of exercise around. But give them an activity to couple with the walk, and it turns into a whole different idea.

So why not let them rock around the block?

This activity isn't recommended for busy urban sidewalks, where passersby are plentiful and injuries are more possible. It also isn't recommended where there is heavy car traffic. Kids who inadvertently kick the rock into the street might chase after it and get hurt by a car. But if neither of these caveats applies to your neighborhood, rock around the block!

The kids each need an item mentioned in Materials. If not precisely one of those objects, something similarly suitable is needed. A ball is *not* suitable, as a round object will roll, is likely to go too far with one kick, and is more likely to roll into the street, down a storm sewer, or somewhere else undesirable.

There are no precise rules here. The general idea is for two (or three—anything more is unwieldy) kids to proceed around the block, each kicking an object in front of him. They may set up their own ground rules, such as having each person kick each rock once in rotation. Jimmy kicks the little gray rock while Seth kicks the smooth white stone. Then Jimmy kicks the

MATERIALS NEEDED:
Two small rocks, stones, pine cones, wood chunks, or similar kickable objects; sneakers

AGE OR SKILL LEVEL:
Old enough to walk around the block without supervision

white stone and Seth kicks the gray rock. Then reverse again, and so on. Or each child can continue kicking the same rock around the block.

It's a lazy, mindless, wonderful thing to do. As the walkers drift to their right or left a bit, separate momentarily and then ease back together, a certain element of cooperation arises as they try to keep their rocks moving ahead of them without seriously breaking the rhythm of their stroll.

Rock on!

WET WALK

On a hot summer day, send your kids out for a Wet Walk! The appeal of this activity is that if the players "win" (cooperatively), they have the satisfaction of succeeding, but if they lose, they have the fun of at least one of them getting a thorough soaking. How many other activities reward you for failure?!

This activity presupposes that you live in either a suburban or rural area, or in a less crowded part of a city. If you live in the heart of Manhattan or Chicago, or in any area where the sidewalks are full of bustling passersby, best read on to another activity.

The two players fill a water balloon and set out for a predetermined goal point—the telephone pole in the middle of the block, the mailbox on the corner, the Masons' front porch,

MATERIALS NEEDED:
One water balloon

AGE OR SKILL LEVEL:
Old enough to walk down the street without supervision

the intersection of Maple, or all the way around the block. As they walk, they gently toss the water balloon back and forth to each other.

The intent here isn't for them to toss it hard, to throw it *at* each other rather than *to* each other, or otherwise deliberately try to burst it against each other. But still, accidents *will* happen. Playing catch with a water balloon is a tricky business at best, and one that builds a wonderful kind of tension.

If the players reach their goal with the balloon intact, they may actually feel a certain amount of letdown, but they'll have the pleasure of knowing they succeeded at something tricky. And if they fail (sploosh!) on a hot day, that kind of failure offers cool, wet, and most enjoyable compensations.

DON'T WAKE ME— I'M SLEEPING

In this simplest of pastimes, one child lies down and says, "Don't wake me—I'm sleeping," then pretends to be asleep.

The other kids then cautiously approach, making noise, even touching the "sleeper," trying to "wake her up." The noise gets slowly but progressively louder, the touches get firmer, as the others try harder to waken the child who's ostensibly sleeping. The sleeper can react to the disturbances quickly or feign deep slumber from which it's hard to rouse her.

But eventually the efforts to "awaken" her prove successful. She jumps up, yelling "You woke me up!" and proceeds to chase the others around the room. The suspense, waiting for the sleeper to awaken and begin the chase, is half the fun for the kids. Is she going to suddenly jump up and begin chasing them yet? Now? With a little more prodding?

The sleeper will quickly learn that it's more fun to wait till the others get closer, perhaps even touch the sleeper a number of times, before jumping up, complaining about being awakened, and initiating the chase.

Once in a while, though, it pays to jump up early, perhaps before the others have even approached particularly close, as this will truly catch them off guard.

The kids should take turns being the "sleeper," unless one child particularly relishes the role and the others all prefer to be chased.

MATERIALS NEEDED:
None

AGE OR SKILL LEVEL:
Three and up

BUTTON, BUTTON WHO'S GOT THE BUTTON?

This is best played with at least five kids; more is fine. You need one person to be It, one to be the Passer. The others stand in a circle or a straight line, while It stands aside and watches intently as the Passer passes the button to one of the other players— and pretends to pass it to all the others.

MATERIALS NEEDED:
A button

AGE OR SKILL LEVEL:
Four and up

The Passer moves from person to person, pausing in front of each of them (except for It). The Passer puts his or her hands immediately over the secretively cupped hands of each player and pretends to be transferring the button into that player's hands. But in all but one case, it's a fake; no button is being passed. Only one player actually receives the button—and it's Its job to try to determine which player that is.

When the Passer has visited every player, he turns to It and says, "Button, button, who's got the button?" It must now name one of the players, who then opens her hands to show whether or not she's holding the button.

Since this is the non-competitive version of the game, there are no penalties or rewards for right or wrong guesses, and the identities of the Passer and It will change with each round regardless of whether It made a right guess or a wrong one. When the round is over, the Passer becomes It, It becomes one of the players, and one of the players becomes the Passer.

THE WINNING ROOM

When the kids want to play a game where somebody wins, yet you're longing for the peacefulness that goes with a non-competitive game, the answer may be a game of The Winning Room. Here the competition is between rooms of the house, not between the kids themselves, so there won't be cries of "You cheated!" or "That's *my* point!" Only the rooms of your house are scoring against each other—aided by your kids, who are working together in cooperation.

Ah, but your kids *are* winners in this game. . . . Winners because they're practicing their alphabet skills. You select any letter of the alphabet; let's say it's "M." Now challenge your kids to find out which room of the house has the most things in it beginning with "M." Going around the rooms together (this is not a contest to see which *child* can find the most things beginning with "M"), they make a list of every item beginning with "M" in each room.

After they've inventoried each room, they count up the items listed

MATERIALS NEEDED:
Paper and pen
or pencil

AGE OR SKILL LEVEL:
Able to spell and write

for each room, declaring the room with the most "M" objects the winner. You can now give them another letter to search for in every room.

Variation 1: Have them only list items that are visible in the rooms. This will keep them from rifling through their siblings' drawers in search of objects, looking into Dad's tool kit (and having an unpleasant encounter with something sharp), or opening your sewing kit and scattering needles around.

Variation 2: Instead of items *beginning with* a certain letter, have them look for items *ending with* a certain letter. This requires a bit more spelling skill and varies the game enough that they won't get bored with it as quickly.

Variation 3: Instead of having them pit room against room to see which has the most items beginning with a letter, have them compare whether a given room—say, the kitchen—has more items beginning with a certain letter or ending with that letter.

Variation 4: Let the competition be between letters, instead of between rooms: Give them two letters, and one room to explore, the challenge being to find out if there are more items beginning with "D" or with "N" in the den, or more items beginning with "T" or with "S" in the family room.

Variation 5: When they're away from the house and in a waiting situation, such as on a car ride or in a doctor's waiting room, have them mentally walk through the rooms of your house, listing the items beginning with a given letter in each room of the house. Again, the "winner" is the room with the most objects in it beginning with the letter you've selected, but their list of items for each room is likely to be shorter, being limited to what they can remember without examining the rooms in actuality.

A TRIP TO PEORIA

If your kids have odometers on their bikes, here's a way for them to impress their friends (while at the same time learning a bit about geography!). With a map of the United States or of your own state in front of you, discuss with your kids interesting destinations. No doubt the kids will hit on Disney World, but you can also take this opportunity to point out sites of scenic or national interest, or places that have personal meaning to the kids. Did Joey's best friend move to Peoria? Are Grandma and Grandpa in retirement in Flagstaff, Arizona, or Boynton Beach, Florida?

When each child has chosen a destination for his or her pretend bicycle trip, help them calculate the best route from here to there, and the distance in miles that's involved. Make a little homemade map showing the beginning and end of the fantasy journey.

From now on, whenever the kids ride their bikes (or maybe at the end of each week, if their daily trips are too short to be significant), show the distance they covered on the homemade map. Did Joey cover twenty-three miles of ground on his bike this week? A colored push pin can be used to mark off the approximate distance covered by each child on his pretend journey to Peoria, Flagstaff, or wherever they're headed.

How long it will take to complete this project will depend on how far each child's destination is from home and how many miles each child covers in the course of a week.

In no way, however, should this activity be seen as a competition to see who reaches her goal first. In all probability, the kids are "biking" to different cities; perhaps Bobby is going to Kansas City where Uncle Ed lives, and Ilona to Anaheim and Disneyland. If anything the kids should encourage each other, maybe even going out for a bike ride together after school to add miles on their respective fantasy journeys.

MATERIALS NEEDED:
Bikes with odometers

AGE OR SKILL LEVEL:
Able to ride a bicycle a reasonable distance from home

RING MY CHIMES

The satisfying *clang* rings out as a horseshoe hits a post, and *both* players look satisfied as they see that one of them has scored a ringer. *Both players look pleased?* Why not? This is non-competitive horse-shoes, and the object is for the two players together to score a combined total of X number of ringers out of Y throws, or within Z minutes. (A ringer, if you're not horseshoe-knowl-edgeable, occurs when the horseshoe lands so

MATERIALS NEEDED:
Set of horseshoes
(including posts)

AGE OR SKILL LEVEL:
Seven and up

that the post lies within the area inside the U of the horseshoe.)

The exact measurement of success in your game is something you will need to determine; a reasonable expectation for one pair of kids might be completely unreasonable for another. Are these seven-year-olds or twelve-year-olds? Are they experienced at pitching horseshoes, or is this their first attempt? You—or they themselves—will have to set the goals: Three ringers out of forty tosses? Five ringers in half an hour?

They can even play to a specific goal with no outside limitations: "We're going to play till we've made eleven ringers between us."

Since this is non-competitive, it doesn't matter who's pitching which colors; each child can even throw one of each color. Only the aggregate total of ringers counts, not who scored them.

GRASS DRILLS

The bane of every high school football player's existence can be the source of a lot of fun for younger kids—as long as they don't know that calisthenics are what older kids do for punishment! The kids will really enjoy the activities, and each in turn will have a chance to enjoy being the drillmaster as well. The drillmaster calls out the orders, putting the players through a series of physical activities of the sort enjoyed (!) by athletes in training. Every child will want a chance to bark out the commands, as all kids like a chance to be in charge and boss the others around!

From two to twenty can play, or as many as your yard has room for. The kids start by lying on the grass face-down. They should be in a single row, side by side, about four to six feet apart from each other. The drillmaster stands facing the prone players and calls out the orders, which can include any physical activity. Here are some standard commands:

MATERIALS NEEDED:
None

AGE OR SKILL LEVEL:
Five and up

Roll right—Roll left. The players roll to their sides, over and over, till the drillmaster tells them to stop. Some clown is bound to roll faster than the child ahead of him and purposely cause a collision, but that can be half the fun of the game.

Crab walk. Lying on their backs, players raise their bodies from the ground and, supporting themselves on hands and feet, move sideways.

Crawl forward and backward. Players move on their hands and knees.

Up—Down. Players rise from prone to hands-and-knees position as quickly as possible. On the command of "Down," they lie down again, or on another command of "Up" they rise to a standing position. From there, a "Down" puts them back to hands and knees, another "Down" puts them prone again, or another "Up" raises them back to standing.

Push-ups. Done in the ordinary manner, they probably shouldn't exceed five in a row unless the players

123

are particularly fit, active, and interested in serious calisthenic exercises.

Burpee (or squat-thrust). The players begin the exercise standing. On command, players drop to squatting position with hands on the ground. Each player then throws her legs out behind, which will put her in the "up" position of a push-up. Then the legs jump forward again until the person is in the squat position. Then the player straightens to a standing position again. The whole sequence is a four-count series of movements, which should be done as quickly and smoothly as possible.

Carioca. The players run sideways, criss-crossing their feet with each step. The movement takes a little practice to perfect, but it can be learned in just a few minutes.

Suppose you're moving from right to left. Start the carioca run by standing with your feet about a foot apart. Now lift your right foot, crossing it in front of your left leg, and putting it down as far left as possible. Now lift your left foot and move it to the left, placing it on the ground in an ordinary standing position. Now lift your right foot again, this time crossing it *behind* your left leg. And now move your left foot to the left again, returning you to ordinary standing position. Repeat, continuing to alternate crossing your right foot in front of and then behind your left foot.

You can carioca back to the right by the same principle, except that this time it's your left leg that alternates crossing movements in front of and behind the right leg.

Sprint. This command is usually part of a three-action command: "Up. Sprint. Drop." On the command of "Up," players rise quickly from the prone position; on the command "Sprint," they sprint forward; then on "Drop," they drop to their stomachs. Obviously the size of the yard will set some limits on the lengths of the sprints. The drillmaster can specify that on the "Sprint" command, players are to sprint forward two steps, four steps, or whatever's suitable.

Forward roll. Players turn a somersault (or several in a row, if room and inner ear permit). Forward rolls can be done starting from a standing position, or coming out of a sprint, or starting in a squat.

Ideally, a forward roll ends with the player up on his or her feet, ready for the next command. For players whose "dismount" position involves sprawling on their backs in the grass, there will be some mixed groans and laughter as they return to their feet.

Frog hop. Players begin in a squat, knees splayed, arms between their knees or thighs, hands in the grass. Straightening their legs, they fly forward, landing in the original position like a bunch of pond dwellers.

Frog hopping is a more exhausting exercise than it might sound. It's well not to overdo this command, otherwise your players might be ready to quit after too many frog hops.

Rocket. Players begin in a squat, then straighten their legs suddenly so as to propel themselves vertically as high as possible. The players' bodies straighten out as they lift up from the grass. Players should be spread out enough that if two players fall over simultaneously, each toward the other, they don't bonk heads. Like Frog Hops, Rockets are more tiring than they sound, and should be ordered sparingly.

Hop. A simple hop can be tiring, yet not as wearing as some of the other activities. The drillmaster can specify "Hop on right foot," "Hop on left foot," or leave it up to the players as to which foot they use. She should definitely specify the direction in which the players propel themselves: forward, backward, right, or left.

The drillmaster can make things deliberately complicated or hilariously confusing by barking out quick changes of orders: "Hop forward on your left foot. To your right on your left foot. Backward on your right foot. Backward on your left foot. Forward on your left. To your left on your right." And so on.

Bunny hop. Players hop with both feet, hands held up but dangling in front of the chest in traditional bunny fashion. (Making buck teeth à la bunny is optional!)

Sit-ups. Another old standard, for which I think no explanation is needed, this is a very popular command with drillmasters.

Drop 'n' roll. Players run in place, facing the drillmaster, until she gives them a sudden hand signal. The direction in which the drillmaster gestures, left or right, will indicate the direction of the roll. Players, on seeing the gesture, immediately drop to the ground and roll over once in the direction indicated, then get back to their feet as quickly as possible and continue running in place, waiting to see which direction they will be ordered to go in for the next roll.

Log roll. This activity requires a certain amount of concentration and agility; it may not be appropriate for smaller children. If nothing else, it should probably be run at half speed till everyone's caught on to the rhythms of the movement.

Three players lie prone, side by side, about four feet apart. Picture Gene, Ryan, and Bob (from left to right), and follow the motions as I describe them. As the exercise begins, Ryan rolls to his left as Gene rises to his feet (probably remaining in a crouch). Gene throws himself to his right, passing over Ryan's rolling body and landing face down, where he continues moving, rolling to his right. Bob meanwhile has risen to his feet, and he throws himself to his left, passing over the rolling body of Gene, landing on

his stomach in the center position, and continuing to move, rolling to his left.

By now, Ryan has risen to his feet. (He's on the far left now.) He throws himself to his right, passing over the rolling body of Bob. As Ryan continues moving, rolling to his right, Gene has risen from the right edge of play and throws himself to his left, passing over the rolling body of Ryan.

And so on. The bodies move like strands in a braid: over, under, over, under; right, left, right, left. It sounds more complicated than it is; once the players know the rhythm, the exercise goes smoothly and looks extraordinarily sophisticated and professional.

A final word about Grass Drills: A person who has suffered and groused through two-a-day practices in muggy August heat will probably not believe that kids from four to twelve actually *enjoy* the strenuous exercise. A former football player or army recruit who has taken orders barked by a coach or sarge may find it hard to believe that kids could enjoy taking orders from a drillmaster.

But kids really get into the active fun of Grass Drills. And knowing that each child will have a turn at being the drillmaster makes taking orders easier; each child knows he'll get a chance at giving the orders soon, if he hasn't had a turn already.

KEEP IT UP

This cooperative effort is the opposite of volleyball. Two or more players bat a balloon to each other, trying to keep it up in the air. For the more competitive or the statistics-oriented, keep track of the number of times the players have hit the balloon, counting aloud each time a player swats at it, or try for each round to exceed the last—that way, any competitiveness is directed at besting your collective previous score, not at outdoing each other.

MATERIALS NEEDED:
Balloon or ball

AGE OR SKILL LEVEL:
Five and up

In the absence of a balloon, you can use a ball—a volleyball works best but other types are usable as well. If you happen to have a volleyball net in your backyard, hitting the ball over the net can be a requirement. (A clothesline also works for this.) But simply hitting the ball to each other and returning it before it hits the ground is ample challenge.

Awwww … someone dropped it. Start over. Can you get up to ten this time? How about twenty? Good teamwork

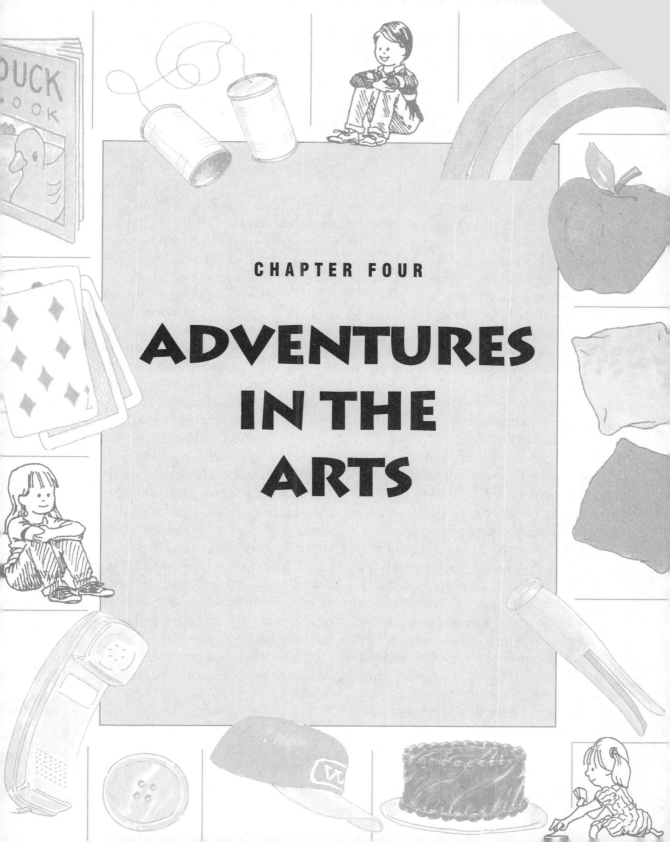

CHAPTER FOUR

ADVENTURES IN THE ARTS

OPEN MIKE NIGHT

Open Mike Night provides a lot of benefits besides a chance for the kids to do something together that isn't competitive. It can be a family activity, an activity for friends—a few or a crowd—or a club activity, if the kids have a clubhouse around which they've organized a formal membership.

One of these benefits is that the shy child can be coaxed out of her shell, encouraged to perform, and given a chance to blossom. Yet another is that the child who has been taking lessons in piano or any other instrument has a chance to demonstrate what he's learned in a more comfortable setting than the yearly recitals the music school may present. And still another is that any child with a natural talent who *isn't* taking lessons, and has no recital at which to demonstrate her talents, can do so here. One more benefit is that the child who doesn't want to take lessons may be encouraged to do so after seeing his siblings or friends performing and getting applause. And last of all, the natural show-off can be encouraged to channel her inclinations into a more socially acceptable means of showing off.

But a child doesn't have to be taking lessons in singing, piano, saxophone, tap, or ballet in order to perform at Open Mike Night (which, of course, can as easily be an afternoon as an evening). The child with a flair for the dramatic can perform a monologue; two together can perform a scene. The child who's a natural ham can stand up and tell jokes. And a child with no other discernible talents can tell riddles or knock-knock jokes. The point is for each child to get up there, perform, enjoy demonstrating whatever talent or ability he has, and bask in the adulation of family or friends.

Who knows—you may even be witnessing the birth of a promising career!

MATERIALS NEEDED:
Whatever the performers need (e.g., an instrument to play, props for a monologue, recorded music, a piano, or other instrument to perform a dance to, etc.)

AGE OR SKILL LEVEL:
Five and up

PUT ON A SHOW

In the immortal words of Judy Garland and Mickey Rooney, "Hey, kids, let's put on a show!" The show can be a retelling of a famous old story, such as *Cinderella* or *The Adventures of Huckleberry Finn*, or it can be an original story written especially for this production. The kids can improvise the script as they go along, as long as all the actors are familiar with the basic story, or they can work from a script.

If not all the kids in your family, or in your child's circle of friends, have the talent and/or inclination to act, one (or more) can write the script, and one (or more) can work on costumes, props, and scenery. Or everyone can get involved in all the aspects, with everyone contributing to writing the script, everyone pitching in and helping with such costumes and scenery as there are, and everyone playing a part onstage.

If you have a video camera, by all means record the show for your future enjoyment.

MATERIALS NEEDED:
Varies according to what show you're putting on and how elaborate a production you want to get into. The actors can be in street clothes, use items from their closets as costumes, or make costumes. Scenery can be nonexistent, minimal, or more elaborate. Props will probably be whatever's on hand. You can work from a script or improvise.

AGE OR SKILL LEVEL:
Five and up

PUPPET THEATER

Putting on a puppet show is great fun, creative, good exercise for the imagination, and totally non-competitive. Kids can work together to put on anything from a retelling of a beloved children's story to a totally original piece of material.

If there's a writer among your kids or their friends, she can write a script for the puppeteers to follow; if not, they can improvise if they stick to a familiar story. Such classics as *Cinderella* or *Sleeping Beauty* are so well known that a script is not essential.

For the child with a flair for writing, an original script is always a possibility. He can either invent a whole new story, dreaming up the characters and writing the script, or he can pursue the "what-happened-to-him/her-after-the-story-ended" line, writing "Cinderella's children," "The Wolf and the Fourth Pig," "Nancy Drew's Newest Case," "Wendy

MATERIALS NEEDED:
For sock puppets—an old sock, rubber band, cotton, buttons and/or marking pens, yarn, glue. For spool puppets—empty thread spool, paint, yarn or crepe paper or cotton, glue, pencil. For theater—card table with sheet over it or any other arrangement behind which the puppeteers can stay out of sight.

AGE OR SKILL LEVEL:
Five and up

Returns To Never-Never Land," or something along those lines.

Now what about the puppets? Of course you can buy puppets in stores, but you can also make them at home. There are simple forms of puppets that even younger kids can make on their own or with very little help. Two of the easiest are spool puppets and sock puppets.

To make a spool puppet, start with an empty thread spool. With colored markers or paints, paint a face. The hair is yarn, glued onto the top of the spool. For a white-haired puppet, use cotton, also glued in place. Another possibility is crepe paper hair.

After breaking the point off a sharpened pencil, glue the pencil into the hole in the bottom of the spool. The puppeteer will hold the pencil—the puppet's body—to make the puppet move. If you wish, you can put clothing on the pencil, either using cloth or construction paper, but this is not necessary.

To make a sock puppet, stuff about half the foot of a sock with cotton (foam rubber or other filling can also be used). The facial features can be painted on if the sock is light in color or white, or you can use buttons for the eyes, sewing them in place. A button can also be used for the nose, if you wish. The hair, again, should be yarn. Crepe paper doesn't work quite as satisfactorily on a sock puppet, and white cotton won't show up as well against a white or pale sock puppet as against a dark sock or a spool, though it's not totally out of the question.

A rubber band around the sock will hold the cotton stuffing in place and create a neck. Cut out two holes for the puppeteer's middle finger and thumb, which will serve as the puppet's arms. The puppeteer's index finger, inserted through the rubber band, goes into the head and works it.

Choose plays that require no scenery or props, if at all possible. In *Cinderella*, for instance, the castle, the fireplace, and so on can all be left up to the viewers' imaginations. And the mice changing into horses and such can be accomplished offstage, indicated by the characters' speech. If the fairy godmother says she's going to change six mice into horses and a pumpkin into a carriage, then waves her magic wand, and Cinderella gasps, "Oh, godmother, you did it!" the audience will get the idea without your kids having to perform magic on stage.

SING ME A SONG FROM THE GOOD OLD DAYS

Along with passing down family traditions and family stories, family wisdom and family sayings, families ought to pass along the songs they remember. Whether these are evocative of a particular event in the family member's life, or of a particular era in the nation, or are simply meaningful because they're beautiful songs, sad songs, or silly songs, almost any song that you (or your own parents or grandparents) remember well or fondly is worth passing down the generational line. If nothing else, it'll give the kids a feel for what music was like in "the olden days."

Whatever the popular songs of your youth were, pass them on to your kids. Along with those you learned from *your* parents—and conceivably from your grandparents, or

MATERIALS NEEDED:
None

AGE OR SKILL LEVEL:
Four and up

ROW, ROW, ROW YOUR BOAT...

other relatives. My daughter grew up with a mix of Sesame Street (the TV's contribution) and show tunes (my contribution), rock (from the radio) and an eclectic assortment of oldies (from her grandma). Whatever music is meaningful to you, feed it to your kids, along with a smattering of other music, especially anything you remember your own family singing to or with you. Preserve those old standards, if only to keep the past generations' music alive within our kids.

The virtues of a singalong *with old music* are innumerable. Of course singing together provides togetherness. Of course singing makes chores go faster, whether it's dishwashing, laundry-folding, or bedmaking. But beyond that, a singalong will leave your child with warm memories.

And if you by some chance can't think of many songs from your childhood and don't have a parent around to teach her generation's songs to your kids, get a cassette of old songs and learn them. It's never too late.

Then your kids, even when you're not around, can sing together. Singing is one of the least competitive, most cooperative activities, especially when it comes to harmonies and rounds. Kids have to actively work on cooperating on harmonies and rounds.

Probably one of the most enduring and simplest rounds is "Row, Row, Row Your Boat." It can be sung as a two-, three-, or four-part round, so two or more kids can sing it together. For two kids (or four singing in two parts), the second singer starts singing "Row, row . . ." when the first singer hits "Merrily, merrily. . . ." For a three-part or four-part round, the second child comes in on "Gently," the third on "Merrily," and the fourth on "Life."

Counterpoint is fun too. Try having one child sing "Pine Cones and Holly Berries" against another child singing "It's Beginning to Look a Lot Like Christmas." The child singing "It's Beginning to Look a Lot Like Christmas" starts first. The one singing "Pine Cones and Holly Berries" comes in on the third syllable of the first song. Now let them experiment to find out what other songs work in counterpoint.

You don't have to be a musical genius or have an operatic voice to have fun in a singalong. All you have to be able to do is carry a tune. And once you adults have taught the kids some new material, you can sometimes bow out of the picture and let the kids sing together by themselves.

But don't give up on the family singalongs either!

AN AUGMENTED CHORUS

Motown's got nothing on your kids when they try a little studio trickery to enhance their own recorded singing. Most kids today own at least one tape recorder—either a "boom box," a smaller cassette recorder, or a larger model. And what child hasn't experimented with either singing into the recorder or playing deejay, if not both. Well, here's a chance for your two (or more) kids to turn themselves into a full-throated, many-voiced chorus through the electronic marvels of technological fakery.

First your kids need to agree on what song(s) they're going to record. They can do a Christmas number, a pop song, an old standard that the family likes to sing together, or perhaps something they've learned in school, in summer camp, or in Scouts.

A little rehearsal is in order first. Then, when they're ready, they record themselves singing the song they've selected. When they play back the recording, if they aren't pleased with the way they sounded, they should consider it a "bad take" and do another—and another, if need be, till they get it down to their satisfaction.

When they're satisfied, now's the time to put that second tape recorder into action. With a tape set up in Recorder 2, the kids play back the tape in Recorder 1 and *sing along with it*. The two (three? four?) voices on tape are joined by two (three, four) more live voices, so Recorder 2 picks up a chorus of *four (six, eight)* voices singing.

And if *that* isn't enough to satisfy them, they can even sing along with the new recording, joining the four-to-eight voices on the second tape. Now they're recording back onto the first tape, and again they're augmenting the number of voices on the tape by the number of live singers. If there are three kids participating, there are three voices on the first tape, six voices on the second tape, and there will be nine voices on the third tape. We're not yet approaching Mormon Tabernacle Choir numbers, folks, but it certainly sounds like more than just your three kids on that tape!

MATERIALS NEEDED:
Two tape recorders, two cassettes

AGE OR SKILL LEVEL:
Seven and up

BAND TOGETHER

Your kids don't have to know how to read music or play an instrument in order to make a semblance of music. They can band together in a band made entirely of homemade instruments.

Play the cigar box by removing the lid, stretching the rubber bands across the open top, and strumming them in the manner of a guitar. Play the water glasses with a metal spoon, striking the glasses with a short, sharp motion to produce the notes of the scale. You can carefully regulate the amount of water in each glass to produce the true eight notes of the scale, or just fill the glasses with different amounts of water and strike different ones at different times to produce pleasing tones.

Whatever else you have in the house that looks likely to produce a satisfyingly musical or percussive sound can be pressed into service for your impromptu band.

MATERIALS NEEDED:
Any of the following—cigar box with rubber bands stretched across it; washboard; eight glasses of water filled to different levels to create the eight notes of the scale; coffee can covered with plastic lid and filled with beads, beans, coffee beans, or other suitable rattly-noise-maker; bells; hardcover book you can make a thumping noise by hitting; comb and can or cup to rub the comb on; pot or pan and metal spoon to strike it with; anything else you have on hand that will make a musical or percussive sound

AGE OR SKILL LEVEL:
Six and up

Of course if any of your kids does play a real instrument, he can lend his talents to the family band and show off his skills with the piano, drums, sax, flute, zither, or whatever the case may be. But a family or group of friends with a total lack of ability to read music or play a bona fide instrument should not let that deter them from a determination to make music—of sorts.

It may sound raucous, atonal, or just plain noisy to you, but what the heck … the kids are having fun—cooperatively!

FAMILY SONG

If your kids ever went to summer camp, they doubtlessly are familiar with a type of song variously known as "comic song," "pep song," or by other names, which pokes fun at the foibles of camp life and the events that go on there.

Consisting of multiple verses, each set to a different popular or standard tune, they frequently are set to tunes whose original lyrics or titles are relevant to the topics of the new lyrics. For instance, a verse about campers not wanting to get up when reveille sounds might be set to the tune of "Oh How I Hate to Get Up in the Morning."

Your family can have its own pep song. Your kids can collaborate on writing their own lyrics to tunes they already know, preferably but not necessarily lyrics whose original songs were relevant to the topics of the new verses. What's fodder for the family song? Just look at the family's foibles, private jokes, recurring situations, and sources of amusement and/or annoyance.

MATERIALS NEEDED:
None

AGE OR SKILL LEVEL:
Eight and up

Does your daughter hog the phone so no one can get through? Does Dad fancy himself a great outdoor cook . . . except that he can never get the fire to stay lit? Did the pet turtle escape, get out into the street, and stop traffic? What about the time that skunk paid a visit? All this—and lots more—is suitable material for the family song.

There are several nice things about having a family song. One, of course, is that writing it is a cooperative project your kids can get involved in together without competition. But another is that hearing the family song, and singing it together, your kids will be drawn together. Oh, sure, they're laughing at each other … and you … and also themselves. But it's good-natured laughter, not derisive, divisive laughter. They're laughing together, not in a way that tears a rift in the family, but in a way that promotes family unity.

PARODIES

Parody in its most developed form is certainly for more sophisticated minds than kids'—you'd hardly expect even your average ten-year-old to be able to, say, tell the story of his summer in camp in the style of Shakespeare.

Ah, but parodies of songs—now, *that* a child can handle!

Kids' parodies can sometimes be crude (and often pretty silly), as in the '60s parody "I Want to Hold Your Gland," or the '50s parody "Take my toe/I'm a stranger in RKO" (from "Take my hand/I'm a stranger in paradise"). But what the heck: the kids have a good time with them. And if their parodies of existing songs don't strike you as gold-medal comedy, that's all right. They're only trying to have a good time, not win writing awards.

By school age—if not sooner—most

MATERIALS NEEDED:
None, or possibly paper and pen or pencil

AGE OR SKILL LEVEL:
Seven and up

kids know about parodies, though they may call them "take-offs" or some other name. Just take the original tune and lyrics, preserve the tune and change the lyrics, but have the new lyrics resemble the original in some way.

Encourage your kids to write parodies of their own.

So what if they sound childish to you—these *are* kids! And, again, they're exercising their creative "muscles" when they write these lyrics.

Who knows—your parodist of today may evolve into a Grammy-winning lyricist in the next decade!

I BELIEVE I CAN SWIM, I BELIEVE I CAN JUMP RIGHT IN.

PICTURE IT— LITERALLY

When I was a child, I was often accused of taking people too literally. But how can a young child help but take words at face value? What a funny world it would be if we all got mental pictures of words with their literal meanings on hearing such expressions as "fencing match" or "drawing room."

Can't you just picture a match wearing a mask such as opponents wear when brandishing foils at each other, waving the sword aloft and saying, "En garde!" Or perhaps your idea of "fencing match" is a match building a picket fence! And as for "drawing room," would that be a room seated in front of an easel with charcoal in hand?

Your kids can have fun by picturing the literal senses of such expressions as "dirty work," "swimming pool," "running water," or "opening night." Depending on where their talents lie, it may be that one child will think of the expressions to be pictured, and maybe even be able to dream up what the literal picture should look like, but cannot express her ideas in a drawing. Another child, though, may

MATERIALS NEEDED:
Paper and pens or pencils

AGE OR SKILL LEVEL:
Seven and up

have artistic talents, despite not being verbally oriented enough to think of suitable expressions to illustrate. Together they're a team, working on the project cooperatively.

On the other hand, if two or more kids all can do each of these aspects of the activity reasonably well, the best thing is for each to work on one or more pictures independently, then trade the pictures around and see if everyone can guess what expression each picture depicts. Some of the sketches that result may even be funny enough to put up on a wall somewhere!

DESIGNING KIDS

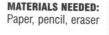

Whether or not you have a budding architect, engineer, interior designer, or inventor in the family, your kids, or your child and his friends, can get together to design things.

What kind of things? Anything from a new kind of school building to a new toy, a home with ultra-modern conveniences to an invention for carrying schoolbooks home more easily. Depending on your kids' ages, the invention or design may be practical or fanciful, one they can carry out immediately, have Dad build in his workshop, or simply dream about.

Whether their inventions or designs are practical, impractical, or purely fanciful, they're using their brains and their creativity, and they're working together to invent

MATERIALS NEEDED:
Paper, pencil, eraser

AGE OR SKILL LEVEL:
Seven and up

or design whatever the current project is. They can literally plan the whole thing together, or one child can work on one aspect while another child works on another.

Who knows—they could even invent the next hula hoop or yo-yo and actually earn money from marketing the idea! Stranger things have happened!

FAMILY SYMBOL

A great collaborative project to occupy two or more siblings is creating a family crest or coat of arms. This need not at all follow the usual rules for such things—you're doing it for your own amusement, not to register it with any official organization. Your kids can devise a crest or coat of arms that they think represents the family, whether or not they know how these things are usually done.

What will they depict on it? Will the family initial be prominent on it? How about Mom's maiden initial? How about a fishing rod to depict the family's favorite weekend recreation? A boat, because someone in every generation in the last four has owned a boat? A book, because the family has always stressed the importance of reading? Wheat to symbolize the farm that was in the family for generations till Grandpa Eddie sold it? Figures holding hands to symbolize family unity? A heart for love?

The crest or coat of arms can be drawn in ink, or the kids can make it colorful with the use of colored fine-line markers. You can also suggest, if you want, that each child draw her personal crest, in addition to working on the family crest.

MATERIALS NEEDED:
Paper and pen or colored fine-line markers

AGE OR SKILL LEVEL:
Eight and up

IDENTI-SKETCH

Even if your kids aren't looking to careers in law enforcement as police sketch artists, they can still have fun with this activity, which bears a strong resemblance to the work police sketch artists do. This is an activity for two kids, one of whom will be the "teller" and the other of whom will be the "drawer." It can also be enjoyed by more than two kids, with one teller and more than one drawer.

MATERIALS NEEDED:
Paper, pencil (with eraser), and any picture of a person's face, such as from a magazine, newspaper, or other source

AGE OR SKILL LEVEL:
Able to draw recognizable pictures

The teller chooses a picture of a person's face from a magazine or other source. As accurately and precisely as possible, he describes exactly what this person looks like: Is it a male or a female? What are his specific facial attributes? Bushy eyebrows that don't quite meet? A short, squashed nose? Medium-thick lips? Short brown hair that parts on the left and is combed flat? A mole on the left cheek? The right eye opened a little wider than the left?

At any point, the drawer may stop the teller and ask questions. Cooperation is essential in this activity, as the drawer is trying to get her drawn face to resemble, as closely as possible, the original, which the teller is describing. It is, however, better if the two players can't see each other's pieces of paper during the process. If the drawer sees the picture the teller is working from, the exercise becomes only one of copying, not of verbal instructions. And if the teller sees the drawer's drawing, it may color his instructions, or he may be tempted to comment on it outright: "You've drawn the eyebrows too bushy." "The cheekbones are too high." "The hairline is too low."

Once everyone is persuaded that all possible detail has been recreated with all possible accuracy, the two pictures are compared. If more than one drawer is involved, there's likely to be a bit of amusement at the way the different drawers interpreted the same set of instructions from the teller.

A note here: The one jeopardy in having more than one drawer take part is the possibility of competition erupting: "My picture looks closer to the original than yours does." But a little parental steering can help eliminate or minimize such comments.

As a side benefit, the participants in this activity will learn—probably without realizing it—a great deal about faces, features, and drawing as they try to translate oral clues into lines and shapes and shades.

Variation: Instead of working from a magazine picture or something similar, the teller, also working with pencil and paper, draws a face out of his own imagination. Then he describes that face to the drawer, who tries to recreate it as above.

OPRAH'S ON

The basic premise here is for one child to pretend to be a talk show host and the other(s) to pretend to be the guest(s) on the show.

There are several ways to play it. First of all, the host can pretend to be one of the well-known hosts—Oprah, Sally Jessy, or one of the others—or she can simply be herself. Then the guests can pretend to be famous people (real or fictional, living or dead), or they can invent people to be—a ten-year-old high wire artist, a seven-year-old whose father is an explorer and who has gone on safari with him, an adult whose life is interesting in some way—or they can be themselves. If you have three or four kids playing, the two or three guests can be "onstage" simultaneously and interact with each other as well as with the host.

The topics of conversation can be serious, silly, or simply creative. If "Oprah" has as her guest a "policeman," the conversation might touch on why crime is rampant and how kids can help prevent it, or how they can protect themselves. Some serious good, or serious thought, might even come out of

MATERIALS NEEDED:
None, except possibly a chair for each participant

AGE OR SKILL LEVEL:
Six and up

this. And if Janet Gibbons (your daughter's actual name) has as her guest Ricki Ryan (her actual best friend), the conversation might turn to "Do kids cheat in school and what should be done about it?" leading to a provocative and helpful conversation on the subject that makes two cheaters rethink their morals.

On the other hand, if "Geraldo" has as his guest a fireman who just got a medal for bravery—as played by your son's best buddy—it may be that nothing will come out of the "talk show" in the way of information, morals discussions, or food for thought, but that's not a necessary outcome; it's a plus when the kids can derive some benefit of this type from the game, but that's not its main purpose. And if the child playing the guest is pretending to be a movie star or pop singer, there too the educational value is minimal, but the fun is great.

Even if the kids don't get into a serious and valuable discussion, this game still stretches the imagination and creativity "muscles."

THANK YOU, AND GOOD NIGHT

Do you think you have the next Walter Cronkite and Barbara Walters in your family? Nurture their aspirations by getting them to present a nightly newscast! And even if they have no such career plans, even if they see themselves as future firemen or nurses, attorneys or rock stars, they can have lots of fun with (and derive some benefits from) this fairly simple yet very engrossing activity. It's one that appeals to the "ham" in most kids, too!

Your part in this venture consists of turning a large appliance carton into a TV set. The carton should, if at all possible, be large enough when laid on its side to accommodate two seated kids (or three) at once. The kids get in and out of it through the open top, now located at one end since the carton is lying on its side.

Your task is to cut a large, TV-screen-shaped hole in the carton. When the kids are in the carton, they will appear to be on TV. You can further the illusion by making the TV set

MATERIALS NEEDED:
One large appliance carton, linoleum cutter or other tool with which a parent can cut the carton; paper and pen or pencil.
Optional: brown wrapping paper or cut-up brown grocery bags, and glue, or wood-grain adhesive-backed paper; crayon, marker, or pen

AGE OR SKILL LEVEL:
Nine and up

look even more real. Ways to accomplish this include covering any writing on the carton, either by painting the whole carton brown or by covering the carton with brown wrapping paper or cut-up brown grocery bags. Adhesive-backed paper with a wood-grain design, though more expensive, will give an even more realistic look. Dials and knobs can be painted or drawn on the "TV."

Of course the kids can perform in many different kinds of shows within the "TV," putting on kids' shows, pretend-movies, or anything that takes their fancies. But what we're particularly interested in here is the Nightly Neighborhood News.

The kids can spend a little while every afternoon (after their homework is done) gathering news from around the family and around the neighborhood. Did the Emersons' cat have four kittens, two of whom are spoken for already and two of whom need good homes? Was there a fender-bender on Jackson Street? Did Mr. Russell back into his son's bike? (Is there a lesson here about not leaving your bike in the driveway?) Did Mom get a promotion at work? All of this is material for the Nightly Neighborhood News.

The kids can actually learn to interview people in the course of newsgathering, learn to sniff out "scoops" on neighborhood news, and learn to write scripts in advance of the "broadcast." Once the "broadcast" has started, they can read their scripts, facing "the camera" (the audience) as much as possible, and interspersing bits of unscripted TV-like patter where appropriate.

The family, of course, gathers in front of the carton "TV" to catch up on all the latest news from your broadcasters.

It may well occur to your kids that no TV show is complete without advertising. If so, they can write their own commercials, either for real or totally fictitious products or services. ("Mom's apple pie—available for a *very* short time. Hurry in or it'll be all gone.") There can be public service announcements too—don't forget to brush after every meal!

SELL THIS!

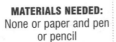

Any number of kids can have fun trying to think of advertisements, slogans, or jingles to help sell outrageous, unlikely, or even unpopular products (the meat loaf special in the school cafeteria?). There's no competitiveness; everyone chimes in with his or her suggestions, and together they can come up with an ad suited to radio broadcast, TV broadcast, or print.

Ads can be for real or imaginary products. How about a package of stick-on chicken pox, guaranteed to get you out of having to take that history test? Let your kids try their hands at writing an ad for that one! (Just dreaming up imaginary products to advertise can be good for a sizable chunk of time before the kids even get into writing the ad copy.)

More creative kids can try their hand at writing old-fashioned jingles; they can take an existing tune (from a song or a commercial) and set new words to that tune, proclaiming the wonderful qualities of the Eisenhower Elementary School Clarion, of St. George's Dragon Repellent, or of their favorite soft drink or candy.

There's a bonus to this activity, too: In the process of writing commercials, the kids may well get to thinking about how commercials are crafted to make a product appealing to consumers, how key words are used to trigger a response in the listeners, and how they, the kids, are manipulated by Madison Avenue. Once they know how they're maneuvered into wanting a certain toy or refreshment for reasons that may not be very valid, they may be less likely to fall for the pitch. An aware consumer is much more resistant to a dulcet-toned announcer or celebrity telling them they should run right out and buy a product.

MATERIALS NEEDED:
None or paper and pen or pencil

AGE OR SKILL LEVEL:
Seven and up

SILLY STORIES

If you've ever played Mad Libs you're familiar with the premise of this game: A story is written with an assortment of words missing. Only the part of speech of the missing word (noun, verb, adjective, adverb) or in some cases a more specific instruction ("a color," "a number") is given, rather than the actual word. One person elicits from the other player(s) a noun, a verb, and so on in the order they're called for, without revealing what the story is about. Then, after words have been supplied to fill in all the blanks, the reader reads the story aloud with the blanks filled in by the words that have been supplied. The results are usually hilarious.

But when you buy a Mad Libs game, you're buying the stories prewritten. To play Silly Stories, the reader has to first write the story himself. The story should be perhaps three paragraphs long. For those of you who've never played Mad Libs, or who played it so long ago they've forgotten, here's a sample Silly Story:

When I went to school yesterday on the (adjective) schoolbus, I was surprised to

MATERIALS NEEDED:
Paper and pens or pencils

AGE OR SKILL LEVEL:
Familiar with parts of speech

find a (noun) in the seat next to mine on the bus. I asked, "Who does this (adjective) thing belong to?" but nobody answered me. The kids in the seat in front of me were too busy (verb)ing and the bus driver was busy with his (noun). So all I could do was (verb).

This (adjective) day continued when I entered the (color) doors of the school and found the principal, a very (adjective) woman busily (verb)ing in the halls. She had brought her (number) children to school with her, and all of them were busily (verb)ing. When I went to class, I found we had a sub, a man named Mr. Johnson, with (color) hair and (color) eyes, who looked to be about (number) years old. He said, "The first thing we're going to learn today is about (noun)." I knew it was going to be a (adjective) school day.

The cafeteria lunch was as (adjective) as ever. The monitor was (adjective) when I cut in line ahead of another kid and (verb)ed me as punishment. The food tasted even more (adjective) than usual, and I couldn't wait to unpack what I'd brought from home just in case, a bag full of (food). The rest of the day was just as (adjective) but the bus ride home was more (adjective) than ever. I was sure glad to get back to my nice (adjective) home!

This game works with two or more players. One is the reader, first writing the story complete with missing words, then calling for the missing words and writing them down as they're called out, and finally reading the finished story aloud, inserting the words that have been supplied. If there is only one other player, she supplies all the missing words in order as asked. If there are more players, each supplies a missing word in turn.

Next time it is a different player's turn to be the reader.

If the kids are stuck for story topics, you might suggest the following: vacations, other trips, new kid in school, first day at work, favorite games, toys, foods, cooking instructions, or a trip to the video game store.

DRAW THAT SCENE

More and more, kids' books are popping up on tape and CDs; some are probably even still available on records. I'm tempted to go into a diatribe here about the sins of letting reading-age kids get their literature aurally instead of by actually reading a book; but I'll restrain myself and look on the bright side: If a child learns to love literature by hearing it, maybe she'll be tempted to read more books herself. (After all, it works with parents reading aloud to kids.) And certainly books on tape are valid for kids who aren't yet old enough to read, particularly if they've got a voracious appetite for stories, one that has them wanting to hear more than their parents can realistically be expected to read to them.

And there's another bright side to listening to books, too: If the kids do listen to them on tape or CD, and then engage in the activity I'm suggesting here, a good discussion can ensue, with some good points made and some good ideas exchanged. The kids will be encouraged to think, to use logic, and to learn to respect their siblings' (or friends') opinions.

MATERIALS NEEDED:
Paper and crayons or colored markers

AGE OR SKILL LEVEL:
Six and up

Let me point out here that if you don't have any kids' books on tape or CD, surely your local library does.

After your kids have listened to the recorded book, ask them to sit down and draw a picture of their favorite scene in the story, and also a picture of their favorite character. When they're all done, spread the pictures out and let everyone have a look at all of them. Ask each child why that particular scene was his favorite, and let each child explain his preference to the family.

Do you see the beginning of a familiarity with public speaking, junior level, emerging here? Do you see the beginning of learning to present a logical argument, too?

A great discussion is likely to erupt around each child's choice of a favorite scene. "But didn't you like it when ____?" "Yes, but not as much as the scene where _____. I liked that because _____."

The kids are likely to interrupt each other, agreeing or disagreeing with favorite-scene choices, agreeing with an interpretation of a scene or saying, "But she *knew* all along that ___." or "He never would have done that if ___." Or even "Doesn't that remind you of the time we went to visit Uncle Henry and ___?"

Let them get into a verbal barrage as long as they're not out-and-out fighting. A good healthy give-and-take of opinions is a good thing; the kids will even get practice in how to disagree with each other's opinions without turning it into a fight. (Your help and guidance may be called for—but don't stop the exchange of ideas, and don't stop them from a reasonable number of interruptions, as long as everyone is getting a fair chance to speak up. Just stop them from calling each other "Stupid" when they disagree with each other.)

Then there are the drawings of favorite characters to look at. Why is this or that character the favorite of one child or the other? And why did they each decide that *this* is how this or that character looks? The kids can get into some heavy discussions on these pictures, too: "What made you think Tom's hair was red?" "I didn't think Uncle Bob was fat—why'd you draw him that way?" "Your Nancy is prettier than mine, but she's too young."

Any discussion that makes them think is good. Any discussion in which they can learn how to exchange differing ideas without fighting is good. Any discussion in which they learn that two people can disagree without one of them necessarily being wrong is good. And any discussion that might lead to a greater interest in books and inspire them to actually want to *read* them, rather than listen to them, is certainly good.

JAMIE'S GOT A HIPPO ON HER HEAD

A certain amount of sibling rivalry—or even rivalry between friends—is inevitable. It can show up in the form of intense competition in games; it can show up in name-calling and other verbal battles; or it can be guided into a gentler avenues of expression, such as drawing pictures of each other in ridiculous situations.

Wouldn't Bobby chortle gleefully at a picture of sister Jamie with a hippo for a hat? Wouldn't Jamie, in return, love to draw Bobby looking silly as can be with a banana sticking out of each ear? Picture Keith with space alien antennae extending from his head, or Seth wearing Grandma's favorite bathrobe.

The kids can surely picture all that and more—and will gladly put it down on paper when you suggest they draw each other in silly situations.

Hint: If the pictures start taking a too-unkind turn, suggest each child draw a picture of herself *and* her friend in a ludicrous situation *together*. Now you're likely to get skies raining chocolate pudding on the kids, or the two of them riding an ostrich or a giant frog, rather than something that might be hurtful. Silliness reigns. So does family harmony.

MATERIALS NEEDED:
Paper and pencil or crayons

AGE OR SKILL LEVEL:
Seven and up

DRAW A WHATZIT

This three-player game has much in common with Very Short Stories (page __). Just as in Very Short Stories, each player takes a turn and passes the folded paper to the next player, and just as in Very Short Stories, no player knows what the player before him has written. But in this game, the players aren't writing stories; they're drawing a picture.

Player 1, utilizing all of the top third of the paper, draws a head and neck. It could be the head and neck of a person, an animal, an alien visitor, or a creature that just took shape in the player's mind but has never before been seen in reality. The player folds the paper so that everything is covered except the very bottom of the neck, showing Player 2 where to pick up the drawing.

Player 2 now draws the upper part of the body, including arms or front paws or hooves, if any, down to the waist or midsection, again folding the paper over so that only the very bottom of two lines are showing.

Player 3 now has to complete the body (below the waist, if the drawing is of a person or humanoid), as well as the feet, rear paws or hooves, or whatever.

When he's finished, the paper is unfolded. You may wind up with a space alien's head on a human midsection and a duck's bottom. You may wind up with a creature whose lowest section is doglike, midsection is that of a cow, and head is that of a unicorn.

What have they drawn? It's a Whatzit!

MATERIALS NEEDED:
Paper and pen or pencil

AGE OR SKILL LEVEL:
Seven and up

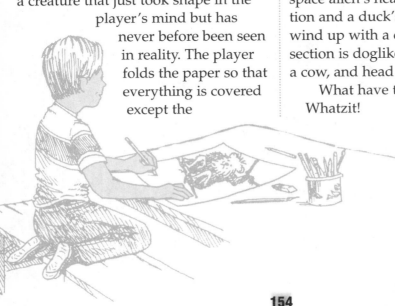

TWO TYPES OF CHAIN STORIES

In both these forms of progressive storytelling, each player contributes one sentence at a time; and in both, the letter each player starts her sentence with is predetermined.

In the first version, Player 1 starts her sentence with any letter of the alphabet. It might be, "There was a full moon shining the night that Jimmy walked over to his friend Burt's house." The next player, however, has to start his sentence with *the letter following the letter that started the previous sentence*. In other words, since Player 1 started her sentence with a T, Player 2 must start with a U. One possibility is, "Under his feet, the autumn leaves crackled." Player 3 now must start with a V: "Very soon, Jimmy got to Burt's house."

You can make a rule in advance, if you wish, allowing players to skip one or more of the most difficult letters—though whether you eliminate only X or also other letters will depend in part on the ages of the players.

MATERIALS NEEDED:
None

AGE OR SKILL LEVEL:
Knowledge of the alphabet

Players continue this way till all the letters of the alphabet have been used (or all of them except the ones you've agreed in advance to skip over). After Z, the next sentence would start with A, and on until you get back to the letter you started with. As few as two players or as many as—well, theoretically twenty-six—can play this game.

The same holds true for the number of players who can play another type of chain story game. In this version, though, the letter that starts each successive sentence is determined not by the order of the alphabet but by the letter that ended the sentence before. Player 1 leads off with "'My pet ostrich escaped!' Jimmy yelled when he saw the open gate." Since he ended his sentence with an E, the next player has to start her sentence with an E. It might be, "Either he ran away or someone rode him out of the pen." In that case, Player 3 needs to start his sentence with an N. "'Now what are you going to do—put an ad under

Lost and Found?' his brother asked." D. "'Don't you think it would be hard for a robber to hide an ostrich?'" H. "How to find the missing pet was the least of Jimmy's worries right then." N. "Not only was his ostrich missing, it had eaten his homework before it disappeared." D. "Dad had promised him $5 if he got good marks on his report card, and failing to turn in his homework wouldn't help." P.

"Perhaps if he called the police they could help." P again.

You get the idea.

In this case, since there is no formalized end to the game, it's over whenever the story has reached a logical, natural ending—or when the kids are bored with the game.

CLIFFHANGER STORIES

It's fun to stick the next person with an impossible situation, or with a half-sentence that dangles enticingly, in this storytelling pastime. Player 1 starts off, telling a story about any characters in any situation that pleases her. It could be a tale of space travelers or a story about a kid just like one of yours, a tale of witches and wizards or a story of a brave third-grader. But not very far into the narrative—preferably at a dramatic or revelatory juncture—Player 1 stops short and turns the story over to Player 2.

Perhaps the story will begin, "Once a boy named Andrew—who hated to be called Andy—was walking down the street with his best buddy. At the corner of Valley Place and Elwood, there was a large carton in the middle of the sidewalk. Overwhelmed with curiosity, the boys couldn't decide whether to open it, but…"

At that dramatic point, Player 1 cedes the floor to Player 2, who has the

MATERIALS NEEDED:
None

AGE OR SKILL LEVEL:
Seven and up

responsibility of the decision: Do the boys open the box?

"Just then a man ran by a block away, yelling, 'He's taken my box. He's taken my box.' Deciding the carton must belong to the man, the boys picked it up and ran after him with it, but…"

It's Player 3's turn. (Or Player 1's, again, in a two-player game.) Perhaps she continues:

"It was too heavy, and the man soon got away from them. The boys put the carton down on the sidewalk. They didn't know where the man had gone. They weren't even sure this was his box. What was in it, they wondered. …"

Player 4 now seems to be faced with the task of telling what was in the box, but of course, he could throw in another obstacle and postpone the revelation. Or the story might take another turn altogether as a fire engine screams down the street, or a bank robbery takes place down the block, or the man reappears suddenly, grabs the box and runs off, or…

These stories have a habit of often changing direction, not to mention location. A story that starts off in the Nelsons' backyard can easily finish on Jupiter. A story about rescuing a princess can easily turn into a tale of rustled cattle.

The game is over when someone—usually someone who thinks the story's gone on long enough—wraps up the loose ends in a few tight sentences, or else when the story just seems to peter out and be going nowhere.

If your kids draw a blank the first time you suggest this game to them,

and they say, "I don't know what to make up a story about," you can suggest they make up a story about a character already familiar to them—a new Ninja Turtle adventure or a new Archie-Betty-Veronica story. But it's better exercise for their imaginations if they make up a story from scratch, and it's good to encourage that without absolutely forbidding derivative stories. Even if they need to be derivative the first time they play, they may well get into more original material as they become more comfortable with making up stories.

COLLABORATING ON A "BOOK"

If one of your children is a born storyteller and the other is any kind of an artist of even modest ability, they can pool their talents on a most cooperative venture—writing and illustrating a "book."

This book can be handprinted in pen or typed up on a typewriter or computer. After it's written, or even during the process, the artistic member of the family can read it, decide what illustrations are suitable, and draw them on pieces of 8½" x 11" paper, the same size as the book is being written on. Later, the whole thing can be integrated, the illustration pages slipped in at appropriate places in the story, and the whole thing assembled into a book.

Two sheets of construction paper, perhaps illustrated and certainly bearing the title of the book and the names of the author and illustrator, make the front and back cover. The pages and covers can be stapled together, or the kids can use a hole

MATERIALS NEEDED:
Paper, pencil or typewriter or computer, crayons or paints, construction paper, stapler or hole punch and yarn or fasteners

AGE OR SKILL LEVEL:
Able to write an entire short story or draw the illustrations

punch and fasteners or yarn to hold everything together.

The writer can choose to make up an original story, or he can write something along the lines of *The Further Adventures of Cinderella*, or *Sleeping Beauty's Kids* or *Pinocchio Grows Up*. If the book is being written specifically for a younger sibling, why not make him or her the star of the story—*Tina's Great Adventure*, or *Chuck Joins the Circus*.

If your young writer is more of a journalist than a fiction-writer—and nonfiction certainly holds an important place in our literature—let her write up an account of a family trip, the story of Great-Grandpa's trip to America on the big boat, or any other true story that bears retelling.

In fact, if your child likes writing but can never think of a story to tell, perhaps he is a budding nonfiction writer and needs to have explained to him that such items as biographies, how-to books, and exposés number among best-selling items in bookstores, and that not being able to think up complex whodunit plots or spy thriller scenarios does not mean a career in literature is out of the question.

If your budding author and artist have a real flair for creating books, and they enjoy putting this one together, they can go on to do many more together, starting a little "library" of their own creations on your bookshelves.

CURRENT EVENTS BOOK

This activity is more of a project than a pastime or game, and I give you fair warning your kids may groan when you suggest it. "Sounds like school!" they may complain, but some schools today don't get heavily into current events, and your kids need a grounding in what's going on in the world around them.

Too many kids are aware of the latest rock icons or movie stars but not world strife, plagues and famines, and political upheavals. Then again, there are the kids who know all the bad news but not all the good news. They think the newspapers are full of nothing but wars and natural disasters, missing the human interest stories completely. True, newspapers play up the global dissension. If a man returns a wallet he found with $10,000 in it, the report of it is likely to be relegated to a small item on a back page. But the kids need to look for these items, too, and know that not all is depressing in the world.

So what I'm suggesting is that they all keep current events books.

MATERIALS NEEDED:
Newspaper, notebook, scissors, paste, glue, stapler, or tape

AGE OR SKILL LEVEL:
Eight and up

Your approach will vary according to the ages of your kids, how much awareness of current events they already have, how much their school does with current events, and whether you receive a daily paper and/or local weekly in your household. But try one of these approaches:

♦ Each child is to cut out one example of "good news" and one example of "the down side" from each day's paper. At the end of the week, the family has a discussion of the week's news, including each child stating what she feels was the single most important news story of the week and why.

♦ Each child is to cut out one example of "good news" and "the down side" from the weekly local paper, as well as one news article that he feels affects him, or your family, directly or indirectly. He then explains, during a discussion, why each of the first two items was important and how the last item impacts on the family.

♦ From any newspaper or magazine, each child cuts out the single most important or meaningful article to him or her that week and explains why that article holds importance for her.

♦ Each child cuts out an article regarding a person he admires or respects. He tells why he admires or respects that person, what the person's accomplishments are, and in what way the child could emulate in his own life the person he admires, now and/or in the future.

♦ Each child cuts out an article regarding a scientific or medical advance, explaining at a weekly discussion why that advance is important and how it might affect her, either now or in years to come.

Note that you can give the kids the same assignment every week from among the suggestions above, or you can request different ones on different weeks to vary the pace and keep them from getting bored. Optimally, the kids will discuss the articles they're poring over and clipping out as they work with the newspaper. In reality, they may discuss the latest Hollywood gossip or the relative merits of rock vs. rap, but even if that's the case, they *are* reading about the world around them and being made aware that it extends beyond school, beyond their friends, beyond their corner, and beyond the glitter of Hollywood. And at the weekly discussions when they offer their choice for most significant news of the week (or best news/worst news, or whatever), they're going to have to *think*.

And through it all, as they work together on clipping articles, though you may hear an occasional "Quit hogging the scissors," you *won't* hear, "It's my turn," "You cheated," or "No fair—that should have been my point!"

COUPLETS

Kids love rhymes, and this simple pastime involves nothing more than one child supplying the first half of a rhyme, then the second child coming up with the other half. Besides being fun, the game teaches cooperation, as the object is not to stump the other player with a difficult rhyme but rather to supply a line that can easily be rhymed with.

Player 1 supplies the first line to a two-line rhyme. Player 2 has to come up with the remainder of this short poem. Since they are working together, it's up to Player 1 to come up with a reasonable first line, one that has the potential for a follow-up and does not end with an impossible-to-rhyme word (such as "orange," which has been stumping poets for years).

The rhymes can be pure doggerel; no one's suggesting the kids strive for

MATERIALS NEEDED:
None, or paper and
pen or pencil

AGE OR SKILL LEVEL:
Five and up

Pulitzer quality. Player 1 might start off with "The snow was falling from the sky," in which case Player 2 could complete the poem with "A snowflake plopped right in my eye." That won't exactly get your kids named Poets Laureate, but the meter works, the lines rhyme, and the poem makes sense—what more could you ask for?

In the process of producing couplets, they'll learn a lot about rhyme and meter and the crafting of simple poems in general. They're working together on a project instead of competing, too. Does it get any better than this?

A BIRD WAS SITTING IN A TREE.

WHEN UP FLEW A BUMBLEBEE.

RHYME FUN

What word, or sound, has the most rhymes? That's a good question to put to your kids, and looking for the answer can keep them cooperatively busy for quite a while.

As I mentioned in Couplets, kids love rhymes. Little ones left playing by themselves can often be heard rhyming nonsense syllables in singsong; rhyme comes naturally to most kids. So most kids will enjoy seeing "which word is the winner"—which word, or sound, they can find the most rhymes for.

MATERIALS NEEDED:
Paper and pen
or pencil

AGE OR SKILL LEVEL:
Able to write

It's probably best if you focus them on a list of perhaps four words to keep them from listing every word they can think of and finding it too daunting a task. You can select the words or let them choose, but four is a good number to start with.

Have them write the four words on a piece of paper, then follow each word with as many rhymes as they can come up with. The list might start out looking something like this:

BLUE	MOON	CAT	WRITE
TRUE	JUNE	RAT	NIGHT
SUE	TUNE	MAT	SIGHT
DO	SOON	GNAT	SITE
MOO	LOON	SAT	RIGHT
COO	NOON	BAT	RITE
BOO	SPOON	CHAT	BITE
NEW		FAT	BRIGHT
YOU		HAT	SLIGHT
STEW		PAT	QUITE
FEW		FLAT	MIGHT
CREW			MITE
CLUE			

That first column seems to be ahead. But after the kids go back and forth a few times, trying to think of more words in each column, they might add a few here and a few there, and a different column might emerge the final "winner." Also, depending on their ages, some of the words above might not appear on their lists. The rhymes the average seven-year-old, nine-year-old, and eleven-year-old come up with are going to be different.

But it's a nice cooperative project that kids of disparate ages can even get involved in together, so if your children are several years apart, this is an activity they can get into together without the age difference being a negative factor.

If they enjoyed putting the first lists together, give them another four words to find rhymes for. Or give them one other and have them see if it has more or fewer rhymes than the word with the most rhymes on the first list.

After they've had enough rhyming for a while, see the following activity for a logical next step.

A RHYME IN TIME

A natural outgrowth of the previous activity (Rhyme Fun) is for the kids to write actual poems. Again, as with Couplets (see page 163), the poems may be pure doggerel, but we're not looking for odes or long, rhymed narratives here. We're just looking for the kids to have fun in a non-competitive fashion.

MATERIALS NEEDED:
Paper and pens or pencils

AGE OR SKILL LEVEL:
Seven and up

This activity, though, is something a little more than just having the kids sit down and write any old poem. After they have several lists of rhymed words, they agree on four and each set out to write a poem from that list of four words. When all the poets are finished crafting their poems, the poems are read aloud, not to

see whose is better but just to see what different poems the kids have all come up with, utilizing identical rhyming words.

There are several options here. First of all, the four words can all rhyme with each other, or the kids can pick two from one list and two from another. Second, the kids can agree on the order in which the words are to appear, or they can leave it open. So the list might read "right, night, bite, bright," or it might read "quite, true, right, new." And the kids can either be free to use the words in any order or be required to use them in the order given. But the rules should be clearly agreed upon in advance.

An example of what a child might come up with from the first list—assuming the words can be used in any order—is

I went out one night
When the moon was bright.
Since that vampire bite
I don't feel all right.

It won't win any prizes, but it does rhyme, make sense, and have a reasonable meter.

The fun is in seeing what different poems the kids come up with utilizing the same words to end each line. Again, this is *not* a competition to see who can write the best, funniest, or most clever poem; it is just an experiment to see what two, three, four, or more people come up with in the way of poems when given the same words to work with as end-of-line rhymes.

TALL TALES ABOUT OBJECTS

Any time you sanction the kids' telling whoppers, they're going to have a gleeful time. And tall tales are part of the American tradition—the stories of Paul Bunyan, Pecos Bill, Mike Fink, and their ilk fill volumes.

But rather than just suggesting that the kids make up tall tales from scratch—which is easier for the more imaginative kids but is likely to stump the others, or at least prove more difficult—why not suggest they make up tall tales *about specific objects*?

The object can be a familiar, everyday object, or something more esoteric. You can have each child make up a different tall tale about the same object, or give each child a different object to tell a whopper about.

"Betty, tell us about the chandelier hanging in the dining room."

"See the chandelier hanging there? It used to belong to the empress of China. Long ago it was a gift from the minister of Burma. He sent it to her on the backs of five elephants. It took them a year to get to China, and

MATERIALS NEEDED:
None

AGE OR SKILL LEVEL:
Seven and up

the elephants ate up a whole forest full of leaves before they got there. At night, when the elephants' handlers were bored and needed something to do, they taught the elephants tricks. After the chandelier was finally delivered to the empress, the handlers and the elephants joined the circus. . . ."

Betty's story was actually more about elephants than a chandelier, but it *did* touch on the chandelier, and it *was* a tall tale. Next, you might ask Craig to spin a different story about the same chandelier.

"Mom and Dad bought the chandelier at an auction. In fact, that was where they met. Dad was bidding on the chandelier and so was Mom. When she outbid him by a million dollars, he decided he'd better marry her. It was the only way he was going to get that chandelier. She rented a U-Haul™ to take the chandelier home in, and he hid in the back and jumped out at her when she got home. He said, "I hitched a ride. Now can I hitch up with you?" They were married the next day, standing under the chandelier in her house. Dad had to put the chandelier up first. She said if he couldn't hang the chandelier she wouldn't marry him, but he did, and they lived happily ever after."

Almost any object can be the focus of a story. A rock? Your son dug it up on an archaeological dig. He was excavating for dinosaur bones when he found the rock, made of a rare mineral that proved to have come from outer space. A seashell? Your daughter brought it up after a dive on which she discovered the fabled lost continent of Atlantis. The blue ribbon on your

other daughter's dresser? She won it when she caught a unicorn, tamed and trained it, entered it in a horse show, and won first prize.

This is *not* a contest to see who can make up the best or most improbable or most imaginative tall tale. There is no competition, no vying for the title of Legend-Teller Supreme. But the kids get a chance to stretch their imaginations while telling lies with parental consent.

"THIS IS YOUR ROVING REPORTER"

What kid doesn't like to ham it up for a microphone or camera? What kid doesn't like to pretend to be on radio or TV? Lend your cassette recorder to your kids and suggest one interview the other—or they debate each other.

Whether one is "Your Roving Reporter" and the other plays a "person on the street" (or a celebrity guest), or whether the two debate a hot topic ("Should school uniforms be mandatory?" or some other subject of interest), they'll have a grand—and cooperative—time at a fun pursuit. And of course, if there are three (or more) of them, one can interview the other two, or all of them can debate each other.

MATERIALS NEEDED:
Cassette recorder with tape

AGE OR SKILL LEVEL:
Six and up

DO YOU THINK THAT DOGS SHOULD BE LET OFF THEIR LEASH IN THE VILLAGE GREEN?

RAINBOW ARRAY

Kids are attracted to color, and they love paints and crayons in varied hues. But how many kids stop to think about the way that different colors are created? Well, they can not only learn but have fun doing it themselves, and then enjoy naming the colors afterward.

As a first experiment, they can put three teaspoons of red paint in each of four empty plastic glasses. Now suppose they add one teaspoon of white paint to the first glass, three teaspoons of white to the second, a couple of drops of black to the third, and two teaspoons of white and a couple of drops of black to the fourth—what color will each cup contain when the contents are mixed? (Tip: To avoid color contamination, the spoon should be rinsed thoroughly after mixing each color, and to avoid color dilution, the spoon should be dried carefully after rinsing.)

Now—what color will result from adding a teaspoon of blue to three teaspoons of red? Suppose they reverse the proportions—a teaspoon of red to three of blue? What does adding a teaspoon of white, or two drops of black, to each of those mixtures produce?

With three primary colors, plus black and white, to experiment with, kids can have tons of fun with color even if they're not very artistically talented. They can simply try different combinations haphazardly, or they can keep strict, scientific-style notes on each container of color, noting what its components are, and in what proportion, so that when they find a color that's particularly pleasing to them, they'll know how to recreate it in the future.

And then there's still more fun to be had when they name the various colors they've concocted—or at least the ones they especially like. Is a certain shade of orangey pink "Maple Avenue Sunrise" (after your street's name), or will they go for the gross (in typical kid-style) and call it "Tomato Barf"?

Either way, they'll be working creatively *and* cooperatively.

MATERIALS NEEDED:
Red, blue, yellow, white, and black paints; plenty of containers for them and for the paint mixtures to be created (plastic glasses work fine here); teaspoon, paintbrushes, and paper

AGE OR SKILL LEVEL:
Five and up

CHAPTER FIVE

MISCELLANEOUS ACTIVITIES

THE SETTLEMENT OF ARZAGON XII

Hail pioneers! Welcome to new worlds, to the intergalactic system, and to the planet of Arzagon XII, home of friendly Ploods and not-so-friendly Deebs … whomever your kids choose, since it's *their* planet and *they* rule it.

Or maybe your kids would rather be Imperial Wizard and Captain of Hyperspace? Whatever—if they create a world, they can take any part in it they want and populate it with whomever they want. Will their new planet be fierce or friendly, with a hospitable climate or a barren one? Recently settled or with a history going back more millennia than books can account for?

The kids can physically construct an area for their planet in the backyard or bedroom, or it can all be in their heads—and perhaps on voluminous sheets of paper detailing the customs and costumes of Arzagon, Mullovia, or whatever their planet is named. Various possible projects include designing the clothing natives and settlers on Arzagon wear, writing a history of the planet (as brief or as lengthy as the kids have patience for), invent-

MATERIALS NEEDED:
Varies

AGE OR SKILL LEVEL:
Nine and up

ing a language, and describing some of the natural plants and/or the foods that grow there, customs of the native inhabitants, weather, natural phenomena, and other features of the planet.

If this is not a planet at perfect peace, who are the warring factions? Is it the inhabitants of one country or continent versus another, or the residents of Arzagon versus the residents of another planet? What weapons do all the warring factions use? Who has the upper hand, and what can be done to shift the balance of power? What incentives for peace can your kids come up with?

What is the structure of life on Arzagon XII? What is the form of government? Does it rule the whole planet, or is each country or continent (or other political division) independent? Does one country have sovereignty over another? Do some of the cultures have more political freedom than others? (Is this a good thing? Why or why not?) Get those kids thinking!

They'll have a lot to think about if they really outline all the complex laws, rules, and day-to-day standards of Arzagon. If they declare the planet one on which no chores ever need to be done, who's going to do the dishes, make the beds, cook the meals, and so forth? The wonderful natives from Squeegax, your kids say? Ah, but do the Squeegax really *like* doing the laundry and dishes and such? For no money? And doesn't that make your child a slave-keeper?

If every Arzagonian has the right to a free flying car, who's to pay for the cars? The government? Where does *it* get the money, then? What if a careless driver repeatedly wrecks his car? Is the government required to keep replacing his car at no charge? No matter how often he wrecks it? Even if the wrecks were due to carelessness, negligence, sloppy driving, or disregard for the needs of maintenance?

All kinds of complex social issues can be explored in the course of discussing how to set up a planet! It requires that the kids fill you in on the details of their planet, of course, if you want to steer the kids to a discussion of social issues, but if you don't, the

kids are bound to realize some of the questions and dilemmas on their own.

Just as the planet can be represented by the backyard, by a blanket laid out on the bedroom floor, or nowhere but in the minds of the participants (and as represented on paper), the kids can act out the part of Arzagonians (and perhaps invaders, traders, or tourists from neighboring planets) or they can merely direct the action without taking any of the parts. The Arzagonians (Patamongians, TerraNovians, or whoever) can be represented by action figures or dolls converted to a new use, or they can be cut from cardboard (a better choice if it's decided that native Arzagonians have four arms, six legs, and two heads), or they can be simply verbalized or written about with no representational figures.

Some more questions the kids may want to deal with: What do Arzagonians do for amusement? What sort of musical instruments are to be found on Arzagon? What do they look like? Sound like? What sports are played on Arzagon? What is featured in their museums? What do the foods taste like? How does the Arzagonian constitution read?

Children who refuse to live in the real world are children with a problem. On the other hand, children who don't have the opportunity to live in a fantasy world have a different sort of problem—they are missing out on an important and rewarding learning experience for which hundred-dollar toys are no substitute.

Welcome to our planet. We think you'll enjoy our cola rivers and the music of the bowda-bowda plants as the wind blows through the forest and stirs the metal leaves. But beware the poisonous zork as you hunt for the snarfru. (Snarfrus are so furry they're cuddly, and they're ideal pets, besides.)

Now what do you want to have on *your* planet?

A HOUSE TO PLAY HOUSE—OR OTHER GAMES—IN

Let me say at the outset to those mothers of boys who wouldn't dream of being caught dead playing house—a sheet draped over a table or large carton also makes a neat fort, schoolroom, office, clubhouse, ship, or other structure. Of course you can also play any of these pretend-games without any sort of structure (in fact, it's less confining), but it adds to the realism if the kids have their own little structure to play in.

If you don't want to retire the sheet from permanent service for its intended purpose, it can be draped over a table, then washed and folded and put away after the game. But if it's an old sheet, you can cut holes in it for a door and/or windows (or portholes, if it's to be a ship). You can also paint windows on it, bushes, a doorbell, a chimney, or whatever other adornments your kids want their edifice to have.

MATERIALS NEEDED:
A flat (not fitted) sheet, and a large carton or table (preferably a bridge table or other table with its legs at the corners rather than one with the legs in the center); possibly scissors and/or paint. Depending on whether they're playing house, school, office, or another pretend-game, they may also want dolls, pencil and paper, your calculator, or other props.

Age or skill level:
Three and up

A discarded carton, of course, can be cut and painted with no repercussions, but as you're less likely to keep it around for very long, you might not want to put as much effort into it. Kept indoors, it'll take up too much space. Left out, it will quickly get soggy in the rain. Still, if you have a large basement, you might be able to store it there for repeated use.

Some of the pretend-games the kids can play in their structure (or without one) are mentioned here, but by no means do they have to limit themselves to those. How about the sheet-and-table or carton becoming a space ship? The kids' imaginations are the only limits.

STEP SCHOOL

Here's a new twist on playing school. Instead of having the child playing the teacher stand at the front of the room, while the other player sits down and pretends to be at a desk, the action takes place on a staircase.

The "teacher" arms herself with a list of questions appropriate to the grade level of the other player (or players).

MATERIALS NEEDED:
A staircase, possibly paper and pen or pencil

AGE OR SKILL LEVEL:
Second-graders and up

These may be written or just in her head. They could be a mixture of spelling questions, state capitals, math problems—anything the player ought to know. The other player—let's assume for now there are only two kids playing, a "teacher" and a "student"—starts out at the foot of the staircase. The teacher asks the student a question. If he answers correctly, he advances up one stair, which is one "grade." Each time he answers a question correctly, he advances one step farther, till he reaches the top of the stairs. When he gets all the way up to the top, he has "graduated," and the game is over.

Now he returns to the foot of the stairs and they trade places; the former student becomes the teacher and vice versa.

If there are more than two kids playing, the game is over when all the students have reached the top and graduated.

WHAT IS THE CAPITAL OF OHIO?

WELCOME TO THE CLUB

To a caveman, a club was what he used when he went off to hunt mastodon for the main course. To a golfer, a club is, a seven-iron, or a sand wedge to get out of a sand trap. But to your kids, or to your child and his friends, a club can be a great source of fun and a sense of "belonging."

Instead of dividing the kids competitively, like some activities and games, membership in a club gives them a sense of togetherness, a feeling of joining together. Of course there's always the potential for dissension in the ranks— disagreements over who's to be president, what activities to engage in—but that can happen with any activity kids get together on. Essentially, though, they're working together, playing together, and feeling united by membership in the club.

What activities the club gets into will depend on the kids and their interests. If your eleven-year-old son and his buddies are the club members, and are all Nintendo fanatics, it's not too hard to guess what the major activity of the club will be. On the other hand, if your kids are ecology-oriented, their club could get into some really worthwhile save-the-earth or clean-up-the-neighborhood projects.

MATERIALS NEEDED:
Depending on the activities the club gets into, possibly paper and pen or pencil, typewriter, fabric, scissors, and glue or needle and thread

AGE OR SKILL LEVEL:
Five and up

What does the club need? Technically, all it needs is a name, a membership list, officers, and an agenda of activities. But think of all the fun if it also has a club banner, a club motto, a club song, a newsletter, a secret handshake, and anything else to make it seem more like a "real" club.

Banner: The kids can use fabric scraps if you're into sewing, or material cut from a piece of clothing that's outgrown and destined for the rag pile rather than for future life as a hand-me-down. If no such item is available, a piece of material can certainly be bought inexpensively at a fabric store. The club's name, symbol, or both can be cut out of contrasting material and either sewn or glued to the banner.

Motto: The club's motto can, but doesn't have to be, related to the club's stated purpose, if it has one. A good general-purpose motto for a friends' club could be FRIENDS FOREVER. A family club might adopt FAMILY

FIRST as its motto. Either one could choose UNITED IN LOYALTY.

If the club is ecology-oriented, a motto might be as simple as GREEN IS THE GREATEST. A club doing good deeds around the neighborhood or community might choose HELP-ING OUR HOME TOWN. Having a motto is not necessary, but like the following items, it fosters a sense of unity among members.

Song: A club song can be a rousing march or something similar to a school's alma mater. Your kids will probably want to take someone else's tune and put their own words to it. Don't worry if it doesn't sound like it's going to win a Grammy; the important thing is, again, to promote unity, along with pride in membership.

Newsletter: If the club really is active, meeting often and doing differ-ent things, the members may want to have a newsletter. This may seem silly for a club of three members who are always together—after all, who is there to report the news to? But if the club is somewhat larger (and even if it isn't) a newsletter is a fine way to recap recent club doings, announce future plans, restate club objectives, if any, and generally bolster the team feeling a club engenders.

Handshake: A secret handshake or secret sign reinforces the feeling of "Oh, boy, this is all ours, and isn't it a big deal!" that kids (and many adults!) truly revel in.

Whatever activities, whatever appurtenances your kids decide on for the club, and whether it's open to only family members, or family and friends, or friends only, a club and its various activities can keep kids occupied non-competitively for many hours of fun—and quite possibly doing good things for the family, the community or neighborhood, or a local charity or other worthy organization, as well.

COOPERATIVE LICENSE PLATE GAMES

A family on wheels for more than five minutes is a family of wiggleworms at best. You may be five hours or five days from your destination, but inevitably one young one will ask "Are we there yet?" not ten minutes after setting out.

There's the inescapable squabbling about who gets to sit up front, next to Mom, or in whatever other seat is favored. There's the whined chorus of "She kicked me," "He punched me," "She poked me first." One child always has to go to the bathroom right after leaving the house, and another will surely have to "go" when you're exactly between two far-apart exits on the Interstate. The car is too hot/too cold, Jeff is thirsty and Bobbi is hungry, and Mom and Dad are ready to tear their hair out.

Ready for a few games to keep the kids busy? You bet you are!

There are lots of games that can be played using license plates. One is Mom's Eating Alligators. Just look at the letters on the plate of any car you pass. Is the plate MEA 675? What

MATERIALS NEEDED:
None, or paper and pen or pencil

AGE OR SKILL LEVEL:
Able to spell

might MEA stand for? How about Mom's Eating Alligators? While the kids may try to top each other for funniest phrase, it's really not a competitive game. No one's judging who's got the funniest phrase. Some of the phrases may strike you as unspeakably silly or just plain stupid, but if the kids are enjoying themselves, and if you've quieted the choruses of "Are we there yet?" how bad can it be?

Another game involves trying to spell names, words, or even whole phrases. Is your family's last name Robinson? Look for the letters that spell your name—but you have to find them in order. Again, a certain amount of competitiveness among the kids is inevitable—each will want to be the first to spot the requisite letters—but as there is no prize for the first to spot each letter, they'll keep it down to a dull roar.

(This game can also be played with street signs instead of license plates if you're driving on local roads and prefer to play that way for a change of pace.)

If you make a list of the fifty states (or the forty-eight contiguous states) before leaving the house, the kids can look for plates from each of the states as you drive along. A check mark placed next to each state as they spot a plate from there will keep track of which states are still lacking.

Again, a certain amount of competitiveness may crop up, with the kids yelling, "I saw it first!" But as there are no prizes for being the first to spot a plate from Montana, Virginia, or wherever, any competitiveness will be slight and should blow over quickly.

How many states you'll spot plates from before the kids give up the quest depends on a variety of factors, but it's unrealistic to expect them to play the game to completion in one sitting. You're not going to spot plates from 48 states in twenty minutes! If this is to be a long trip, put the paper aside and pick it up again later, or tomorrow if it's a multiday trip.

Other license plate games include looking for the digits of your address and phone number, the birthdates and ages of all the kids in the car, or the birthdates of all the occupants, adults and children alike, or any other relevant numbers.

"WHAT YOU GOT THERE?"

I include this game in this book even though there's a streak of competition in it because it's of such a mild nature that it almost doesn't count. Nobody is trying to win anything here, but each child is trying to make the other show her teeth first!

As with many other childhood pastimes developed by kids themselves, the continuity of this game is somewhat baffling. The initial dialogue of the game has no bearing on the game itself, which comes after the dialogue. The child who decides to play this game initiates play by asking the second child, "What you got there?"

The second child—assuming he has played before and knows the routine—responds, "Bread and cheese." From there, the dialogue goes:

"Where's my part?
"Mouse got it."
"Where's the mouse?"
"Cat got it."
"Where's the cat?"
"Hammer killed it."
"Where's the hammer?

MATERIALS NEEDED:
None

AGE OR SKILL LEVEL:
Six and up

At this point, Player 2 has to invent the forfeit for the game. The initial part of the response to "Where's the hammer?" is invariably "Behind the kitchen door cracking nuts, and the first one to show his teeth has to _____." It is in finishing the sentence that Player 2 shows his ingenuity—or fiendishness.

The forfeit may be simple: Sing "Oh Susannah." Recite the alphabet backward. Drink a glass of water quickly. Stand on your head. Walk around the outside of the house backward.

The period between revealing the hammer's whereabouts and having the forfeit acted out is likely to be fraught with goofiness as each player tries to make the other reveal those pearly whites. But be careful, kids, in making faces to try to make the other player laugh—if you don't watch out, you'll show your own teeth!

The game can be played in virtually any situation where silence is not the rule. It's as appropriate on car trips as it is in filling time at home. The forfeit in a game played on a car trip would obviously have to be of the backward-alphabet or other inactive variety, suited to being performed while seated in the car. (Other car-suited forfeits include "Make a noise like a pig," or "Say 'I'm a nerd' five times." But the game, with allowances for situation, is adaptable to most any setting—though not in class or during church services!

FINE OR SUPER-FINE?

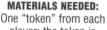

This game can be played by as few as two players or by quite a few more. Each player contributes a "token" to the "pool." Each token is something that belongs to a player, is recognizably hers (that is, two people shouldn't each contribute a yellow pencil or a white sweatsock), and won't give away its identity by sound (such as keys that would jingle). The pool is simply a bowl, a table, a chair, or another location central to where the game is to be played, where all the tokens can be deposited together.

The player who is "It" sits facing away from the pool of tokens. The other player selects one token from the pool and holds it over the back of Its head, out of sight, intoning, "Heavy, heavy hangs over thy head."

It replies, "Is it fine or super-fine?"

The player holding the token answers, "That remains to be seen; what shall be done to redeem it?"

Now It has to make a decision. The task required for redemption may be comical (kiss the fencepost) or truly rewarding (eat a square of chocolate). The owner of the object being held

MATERIALS NEEDED:
One "token" from each player; the token is any object that recognizably belongs to that player

AGE OR SKILL LEVEL:
Nine and up

over Its head will have to perform the task in question—but is the owner of that token It or the player holding the token?

It could say, "Draw a funny face for the amusement of the others," knowing he is a good artist and will get accolades for his comic sketch, and if It himself is the owner of the token, he will have an enjoyable chance to do something he likes.

Redemption tasks should be pleasant and enjoyable or comical and humorous, without ever veering into the realm of unkindness, humiliation, or danger. Each player takes a turn at being It in rotation, without regard to the outcome of the previous Its turn.

WHAT'S COOKIN'?

Another great project in which to harmoniously involve all the kids in one family is writing a family cookbook.

A family cookbook can be comprised of the kids' favorite recipes that they like to cook themselves, their favorite eating from among Mom's or Dad's recipes, "heirloom" recipes from among the extended family, or some of all of these.

How you divide the book, if you do, is optional. If it's a small book of ten recipes, you don't need to divide it at all. If, on the other hand, it encompasses some forty or so recipes, you might want to divide it into sections.

These might be traditional divisions such as "Appetizers," "Main Courses," "Snacks," and "Desserts." Or it could be "Heirloom Recipes," "Mom's Best," and "Kids Can Cook Too." Or pick any other set of sections that works for you. After all, it's *your* book.

The kids' contributions to creating this cookbook can include any or all of the following: writing down all their favorite recipes that they can cook themselves, agreeing on which of your recipes should be included, interviewing other family members—grandparents, aunts and uncles, cousins—to get their best or favorite recipes, neatly printing or typing the recipes and stapling them together between two pieces of construction paper, which can serve as the covers.

If the kids want, they can even make copies of the cookbook (by using a photocopier, or by running out multiple copies from a computer). It can then be distributed to other members of the extended family.

Whether your kids create a cookbook filled with such basics as variations on Jell-O, or whether some truly sumptuous feasts find their way between the covers of the book, they'll have a good time working harmoniously on the book itself, and afterward the book is likely to inspire some equally non-competitive kitchen activity.

And the results of *that* are likely to be delicious for all the lucky beneficiaries!

MATERIALS NEEDED:
Paper, pen or typewriter or computer, one sheet of construction paper, stapler

AGE OR SKILL LEVEL:
Able to write and spell, with some cooking skills

BAKABLE FUN DOUGH

Your kids can make a-dough-rable figures they create and bake themselves, or simple stars and moons for the younger or less artistic set, with this bakable fun dough recipe.

First prepare the dough as follows: Mix the salt, flour, and water together, adding the water a little at a time, and using a little more or less than two cups, as needed, to make the dough easy to handle. When it's well mixed, knead it with your hands until it's smooth. Roll it out on waxed paper, using a rolling pin, till it's a half-inch thick.

Cut the shapes you want from the dough. You can use cookie cutters to make moons, hearts, or whatever shapes you have available. You can use a knife to cut out other figures. You can use

MATERIALS NEEDED:
Measuring cup, mixing bowl, mixing spoon, waxed paper, rolling pin, cookie sheet, cookie cutter(s) and/or knife, spoon, toothpick, 2 cups salt, 2 cups (more or less) warm water, 5 cups flour, paint, clear shellac, paintbrush

AGE OR SKILL LEVEL:
Nine and up, or younger with more parental help

the end of a spoon's handle to make a mouth if you're creating figures and want to give them faces. A toothpick, stuck into the dough and twirled around slightly, makes eyes. Sculpt the shape of the nose with a knife or other tool.

If any of the shapes are going to be hung, poke a hole in those shapes by inserting a toothpick, then wiggling and twirling it till the hole is large enough for string, twine, or ribbon.

When all your shapes are complete, place them on a cookie sheet and bake at 300°F for an hour. After they cool, they can be painted, if desired, and covered with clear shellac.

CLIPPING COUPONS ...OF A SORT

When the kids put their heads together to dream up the contents of the coupons they're going to create, you lucky parents are going to be the recipient of more than just a blessed period of non-squabbling. Technically this is an activity that one child can engage in just as easily, but when two or more siblings get together, they can spark ideas in each other, make suggestions, and get together on the benefits to be offered on their coupons.

So what are these coupons?

They look like the coupons that are offered by mail or in the local paper. But instead of offering ten cents off on a box of cereal, or a free hour at the local tanning salon or bowling alley, these coupons offer you something far more valuable. Examples:

- THIS COUPON REDEEMABLE FOR ONE CLEAN BEDROOM ON DEMAND.
- BEARER MAY REDEEM THIS TO GET THE DISHES DONE BY ANDREW ON ANY EVENING.

MATERIALS NEEDED:
Paper and pen, crayons, or markers

AGE OR SKILL LEVEL:
Able to write and do simple household chores

- GOOD FOR ONE OFFICIAL HUG FROM ANNIE.
- THIS COUPON CAN BE EXCHANGED FOR ONE HALF-HOUR OF GUARANTEED SILENCE BY BOTH KARI AND TRACY.
- GRANT WILL WASH THE DOG ON SURRENDER OF THIS COUPON.

The kids can work out, among themselves, the offers to make in the coupon book, and you parents will enjoy cashing in on the benefits. The kids might even learn something about life in the course of creating the coupons, about how cooperation has a good effect on your life, about the importance of honoring personal commitments—even when it's unpleasant, distasteful, or difficult to do so.

The kids' coupons can all be stapled together, with the coupons torn off and redeemed at your discretion.

CHIPS AHOY

Kids in the younger age ranges can have a heck of a good time with nothing more than a rack of poker chips. It doesn't matter if they're the conventional plastic chips that have been around for several decades, or something older that's been in the family for a few generations—leather, cardboard, or even the old clay variety. The kids can have a good time in a most cooperative manner.

MATERIALS NEEDED:
Poker chips

AGE OR SKILL LEVEL:
Three and up

- Dump all the chips in a big pile and have the kids put the chips back into the slots, sorting by color.
- Again dumping the chips out first, let the kids replace them not with all the blues together, all the whites, and all the reds, but in some pretty pattern visible through the openings.
- Let the kids play "store" and even make change if they're old enough, paying two blue chips for a make-believe apple or six white chips for a pretend quart of milk, and perhaps getting chips back as change according to whatever rules you've worked out as to value.
- If these are the modern plastic poker chips with milled edges, the kids can scrape the ridges together and make a most satisfactory (to them if not to you!) noise.
- They can roll them across the floor, seeing how far they can get any chip to roll. They can experiment to see on which types of surfaces the chips will roll the easiest, the farthest, and along the truest straight line. Though of course you know the chips will roll better on wood than on carpet, better on flat linoleum than on raised linoleum, and better on flat tiles than on concrete, this seemingly evident fact may not be so obvious to your five-year-old, so let her find out for herself.

- They can flip chips off their middle fingers, using their thumbs, and try to see how far it's possible to flip a chip.
- They can flip one chip, then try to see if they can flip another to the same place, so it touches the first chip.
- Two kids can flip chips into the air simultaneously and see if they can get their chips to "crash" together.
- One child holds a hoop-shaped object in the air. The other child, standing a reasonable distance away, tries to flip chips through the hoop. (If you have nothing else suitably hoop-shaped in the house, you can pull a wire coat hanger apart into some semblance of a hoop, taping the pointy end so the child is protected from accidental injury.)

- Dump a quantity of chips in a paper bag, one for each child, and have them shake the bags rhythmically, perhaps in time to some music you put on the stereo. It's poker percussion, folks!
- Have each child balance a poker chip on the eraser end of a pencil (or on the tip of his finger). If *both* kids (all the kids, if there are more than two) can take six paces forward without dropping their chips, they all win a small prize (such as a handful of raisins).
- And finally, have the kids make a list of other activities they can think of to do with the poker chips. (If they're too young to write, you keep track of the ideas.) This will give them even more things to do with the poker chips next time.

CONSTRUCTION CHIPS

Another activity in which poker chips can be used to amuse kids for long periods on end is construction. It's an odd yet true fact that a child who has played with a set of building blocks till she's bored with them can be handed a different type of construction set and happily turn right around and start building all over again.

The idea behind using poker chips to build towers is that the kids can construct colorful structures—all sorts of mixtures of red, blue, and white chips. Your kids can intermix the colors at random, of course, but how much more fun to use the layers of color deliberately.

They can alternate red, blue, white, red, blue, white through the whole structure. They can change the pattern halfway up, or construct the top and bottom of the structure out of one pattern and the middle out of a different one. The pattern possibilities are endless.

If they build two columns touching each other (and don't build them too precariously tall), they may be able to extend a third column, based half on each of the two lower columns, up from those two to reach impressively ceilingward. Simply building a stack for height can be fun, too. Disregarding (if they want) the aesthetics of the tower, ignoring color composition, your kids may simply take turns stacking chip after chip on the tower, seeing how tall it will go before it precariously teeters, wobbles, and crashes to the floor.

Not all structures have to be tall, either. A pleasing pattern of chips on the floor, perhaps three chips tall, perhaps in a single layer, can be laid out to resemble the boundaries of perhaps a large building, a neighborhood of individual buildings, or a city for your daughter's smaller dolls to "live in"? Your kids can even have fun just constructing random or planned patterns of the different colored chips on the floor (or on a table).

Even if your kids don't have a future in architecture, they can have a great time *now* building with poker chips!

MATERIALS NEEDED:
Poker chips

AGE OR SKILL LEVEL:
Four and up

BUILD A CITY

Though kids love to build houses or skyscrapers using blocks, toy logs, or whatever other kits are available, two kids each building a structure aren't really working *together* at their construction. If, however, they build a city together, their play becomes not only non-competitive but out-and-out cooperative.

And there are so many things besides just blocks and logs that can be used to construct a city. Of course the traditional building toys can be used, but why should they restrict themselves to just those? All the items listed above under Materials are applicable to the building of bridges, tunnels, caves, tall buildings, or any other kind of structure the kids might want to have in their city.

Will they build roads, too, or just have imaginary roads? Will this chair be an observation tower, a tall building, or a ranger lookout station in a forest on the outskirts of the city?

There are all kinds of possibilities. All that's needed is a healthy imagination and the creativity to dream up the possibilities and put them into action. Imagination can plan a splendid city, and teamwork can build it.

MATERIALS NEEDED:
Chairs, empty wastebaskets, empty boxes, books, pieces of cardboard, and whatever else presents itself as likely "construction material"

AGE OR SKILL LEVEL:
Four and up

WHITHER THE WEATHER

There are actually a number of different projects the kids can get into that involve comparing the weather across the country. For starters, each child can pick one or two cities he wants to track the weather of for the next month. These might be a relative's city, the city nearest the town where the kids went away to summer camp, the city nearest where your daughter's kindergarten friend moved to, or a city familiar to your kids from a book, TV show, or movie.

In the first column on each city's sheet of paper, the child writes the dates for thirty consecutive days. (You may be starting this project in the middle of a calendar month, and running into another month—that's no problem.) In the second column, he writes the high and low temperatures for that date as reported in your local paper. And in the third column, the weather for that date—sunny, partly cloudy, cloudy, rain, snow, sleet, etc.

MATERIALS NEEDED:
A map of the United States or, preferably, of North America, the daily paper's report of weather in other cities across the country, paper, scissors, removable tape, pen or pencil, and for each city being tracked, a piece of paper divided into three columns across

AGE OR SKILL LEVEL:
Seven and up

After a month, he has a fair idea of what the weather's likely to be at that time of year in that city, or those cities, that he's been tracking. He can also compare those figures to the statistics his friends or siblings have compiled for the cities they chose.

Another activity involves watching the weather map in the paper each day as it shows the highs and lows. Your kids can cut out small circles with an H or L written in each, representing highs and lows. Your kids tape H's and L's on their own maps, wherever today's newspaper shows highs and lows occurring. If the newspaper indicates rain, snow, sun, or other conditions, your kids can tape circles showing those conditions to their maps as well.

Tomorrow, when the paper shows the latest highs and lows, the kids move their circles accordingly on their own map, and from this they'll get an idea of how weather patterns move, how the weather generally proceeds from west to east, where it's likely to be raining tomorrow if it was raining in Topeka today, and what the weather's likely to be in your city tomorrow. Of course they won't always get it right, but neither do the professional forecasters!

If you have a source for reports of world weather, the kids can track a global map and see what the temperatures and weather conditions are around the world. They'll learn, if they don't know already, that when it's summer in the Northern Hemisphere it's winter in the Southern Hemisphere, and while we're dreaming of a white Christmas, Aussies are water-skiing.

You can discuss latitude, the Gulf Stream, and the proximity of moun-

tains or large bodies of water to the location in question. There's also the jet stream and altitude. You can go to the library and get some books. Even if you don't understand all these factors and the way they affect weather, or feel your kids aren't old enough to understand them, you can explain the ones you do understand and feel they can grasp.

Any other weather-related activities you can think of to involve your kids in will also make them more aware of the weather differences from city to city or from season to season, or the movement of weather patterns across the country or even around the world.

OBSERVATION TEST

Two kids can test each other's powers of observation. One studies the other for thirty seconds. Then the one who was being studied leaves the room and changes five things about her appearance. She might unbutton a shirt's top button, roll up sleeves, put on or take off a belt, put her shoes on the wrong feet, put on or take off a piece of jewelry, part her hair in a different place, or otherwise change her appearance.

MATERIALS NEEDED:
Whatever the child is wearing

AGE OR SKILL LEVEL:
Five and up

Returning to the room, she asks her friend to find the five things she's changed. (If she can only think of four, or can think of six, that's fine, but she needs to tell her friend exactly how many changes she's made.)

Then the friend does the same thing, testing the first child's powers of observation.

BOBBING FOR APPLES

A traditional game of the good old days, especially popular around Halloween, Bobbing for Apples isn't nearly as popular as it used to be. Why? Could it be that at parties people are reluctant to put their faces and mouths into water other people have had their faces and mouths in, and to bite on apples others have bitten on?

Well, that's certainly no reason not to play it with your own family!

The game is simple: Fill a large pot or tub with water. There should be enough water that apples will float and won't touch bottom immediately if pushed down a little. Now put a number of apples in it—at least as many as there will be people playing.

Each player in turn, with hands behind back, now sticks his face into the water and tries to latch onto an apple using only his teeth. When everyone has an apple, the game is over and the chomping and crunching begins. Everyone's a winner—and the prize is so healthy for you, too!

MATERIALS NEEDED:
Large tub, pot, or other container, preferably one that is very wide but not too deep (it must be big enough for someone to put his head into with room to spare); water; apples

AGE OR SKILL LEVEL:
Four and up

MAKEOVERS— ON PAPER

Despite the revolution that proclaims boys can play nurse, can play kitchen, can play with dolls, and girls can play cowboys, can play construction workers, can play with military toys, there are still some activities that are only likely to appeal to one sex or the other.

This is one of them; I doubt very much that many boys are going to be interested in playing Makeovers, probably not even those who are headed for careers as fashion designers or Hollywood makeup artists. But many girls will love it. Girls are more likely to be into fashion, into hairstyles, into makeup. And the next best thing to putting on grown-up clothes and makeup themselves is to dress up dolls or draw beautifully coiffed, brightly made-up faces on paper.

If your daughter and her friends have seen the "makeovers" featured in fashion magazines you or their friends' mothers may have around the house—or even if they've never seen such a feature in a magazine—they're likely to jump on this activity

MATERIALS NEEDED:
Lightweight paper, pen, crayons, colored pencils or markers

AGE OR SKILL LEVEL:
Nine and up

as sounding like lots of fun. The premise is that the girls first draw a woman in need of a makeover, then draw her again in her "new and improved" state. The original can be drawn in pen; the "madeover" version will do better in crayons or markers or colored pencils, so that the eye shadow, lipstick, hair, and perhaps even blusher can be drawn in color.

The purpose of using lightweight paper is as follows: Once the original picture has been drawn, the basic features and head should be drawn over again as a base for the makeover picture. This can be most easily accomplished by putting lightweight paper over the original and tracing. But if your kids can copy the original fairly accurately onto another piece of paper without tracing, the requirement for lightweight paper can be dispensed with.

On the "makeover" picture, the girls are free to make any improvements they see fit. This does not include giving the faces a nose job! These makeovers are not "before" and "after" shots of plastic surgery patients. But the lips can be thickened slightly, as can be done with lipstick; they can be colored any color that lipstick might be. The eyes can have heavy liner, thin liner, or no liner drawn. The eyebrows can be made bushier, bolder, or even finer (as if plucked), the hair can be styled differently; the lashes can appear mascaraed.

♦ If the girls want, they can draw whole figures instead of just heads, and the makeovers can include clothing as well as hairstyle and makeup.

♦ If they want, each girl can draw both the "before" and "after" of each face, then pass the pictures around to show the others. Or each girl can draw a "before" picture, then pass it, along with the bare sketch that will be the foundation for the "after" picture, to her friend (or one of her friends, if more than two are playing). The other girl then does the makeover, while the first girl makes over the face drawn by the other girl.

TIN CAN TELEPHONE

This most cooperation-inducing toy is probably as old as tin cans (which are no longer made of tin) themselves. I don't know who was the first parent or child to discover that a length of string connected to two empty cans will carry sound crudely from can to can, but it does, and someone discovered it, and kids have been playing with tin-can telephones ever since.

An adult is needed to drive a nail through the middle of the closed end of each can and to slip the length of string through the resultant hole in each can. A knot is then tied in each end of the string, which in each case will be inside a can. Your kids now have a crude telephone. If one talks into one can while the other listens to the other can, the listener will hear the talker, even if he goes around a corner and lowers his voice so it doesn't carry any way but through the string. Don't expect clear tones and perfect reception, but it's a fun toy.

You can't listen and talk at the same time, as the can has to be next to the listener's ear and the speaker's mouth to work right. Therefore your kids may want to resort to the old system of saying "Over" at the end of a thought, signaling that the listener is now free to remove her can from her ear and put it to her mouth, while the former speaker now puts his can to his ear to listen.

It's not as high-tech as a walkie-talkie with all the bells and whistles, but in its very simplicity and crudeness, it has a certain charm that can't be denied—and the price is very right!

MATERIALS NEEDED:
Two empty cans with their lids removed, washed clean, and examined to be sure there are no sharp edges; length of string at least 10 feet; nail; hammer

AGE OR SKILL LEVEL:
Four and up

CLOTHESPIN DROP

Another goofy game that kids will giggle over, Clothespin Drop is hard to score in but easy to have fun with. It's also about as simple a game as you could wish for.

A wide-mouthed quart jar is placed on the floor, open end up. One player at a time, in turn, stands next to the jar. She tips her head far enough back to rest an ordinary clothespin on the forehead or the bridge of the nose, closing her eyes so there's no danger of the pin slipping into the eyes. She then tips her head slowly forward till the clothespin slides off and drops—hopefully into the jar.

Any number of kids can play. No attempt is made to keep track of any score, per player or cumulative. Each player takes one turn at a time, regardless of whether she succeeds or misses. The game is over when the players decide to go on to something else.

MATERIALS NEEDED:
Clothespin, wide-mouthed quart jar (such as a mayonnaise jar or canning jar)

AGE OR SKILL LEVEL:
Six and up

HAT TRICK

Like Clothespin Drop, this game is fun to try your hand at but needn't be played competitively. Two or more kids can have fun just trying to flip cards into a hat (or similar receptacle) without any attempt made at scoring. Everything in this life doesn't have to be a who-won? situation. Sometimes it's nice to play for the sheer fun of playing or of trying to succeed, with no mind to how well one's opponents are doing in comparison.

Players stand, sit, or kneel about four feet from the hat. Each player can hold his own deck of cards, or one deck can be divided between or among the players. The object of the game is to propel the cards through the air in such a way as to make them land in the hat (or other receptacle). The problem, of course, is that a tossed or flipped playing card flutters unpredictably and uncontrollably. A gentle flick of the wrist can send a card zooming in bizarre directions.

The players can take turns flipping their cards, or several can flip card after card at one time—creating yet another obstacle to scoring a goal, as your card might be headed dead-on for the hat only to be knocked off course by another player's card.

Players can congratulate themselves with each card that goes into the hat, or everyone can wait till all the cards have been flipped, then count the number of cards in the hat and congratulate themselves all-inclusively on the grand total of cards that landed where they were supposed to, regardless of which players put how many of them there.

MATERIALS NEEDED:
A hat, mixing bowl, saucepan, or empty wastebasket; a deck of cards or two, or a stack of 3 x 5" index cards

AGE OR SKILL LEVEL:
Five and up

FLOATING RAINBOWS

Mix the detergent, glycerine, and water, and presto—you have bubble solution without having to pay retail prices for it. If you already have two (or more) bubble wands in the house—one for each child who'll be playing—great. If not, you can improvise with a couple of pairs of eyeglass frames minus the lenses—great for releasing two bubbles at once from each wand—or coat hangers bent into more or less of a circle—great for giant bubbles! Or use any other suitably shaped objects you have around the house.

Then watch those bubbles float into the sunlight, with rainbows glistening in them as they hit the right angle.

MATERIALS NEEDED:
½ cup liquid dish detergent, 2 tablespoons glycerine, 5 cups cold water; covered plastic container for storing leftover bubble solution; bubble wand from the store (or make your own from a coat hanger, or a pair of eyeglass frames minus the lenses, or any other suitably shaped object); frying pan or similar large, shallow container if you use a coat hanger for a bubble wand

AGE OR SKILL LEVEL:
Three and up

DRAWBACKS

This simple pastime amused us as kids and can keep your kids occupied peacefully, too. It's as good for a two-minute interlude as for a more protracted game. And all that's needed is one child's index finger and another child's back. (Only two can play at a time, but if more than two kids want to play, the others can wait their turns, since turns are short.)

Player 1 announces "Picture" or "Word," then with her finger either "draws" a simple picture or "spells" a word on the other child's back. If it's a picture, it should be something very simple. If it's a word, block capitals should be used to spell it.

The player whose back is being drawn on has as many chances as he wants to guess what the picture or

MATERIALS NEEDED:
None

AGE OR SKILL LEVEL:
Six and up

word is. Since there is no winning or losing this game, the player can guess till he gets it right or gives up. The player doing the drawing can give hints if she wishes. If the player who's doing the guessing gets words right consistently, the player doing the drawing can "graduate" to spelling out whole sentences.

Normally the players take turns doing the drawing and the guessing, but in rare cases one player greatly prefers doing the drawing and is playing with one who greatly prefers doing the guessing. In this case, there's no harm in letting each always take the part she likes, since there is no competition, no winner and loser, and therefore no actual need to give each player an equal number of turns at drawing and at guessing.

SECRET MESSAGES

If your kids get good at Drawbacks, they can send each other silent messages, drawn on each other's back. One child spells out a word on the other's back; the recipient "reads" the first child's "writing" and in that way gets the message.

A few hints:

♦ Use capital block letters, not lower case or script.

♦ Spell slowly.

♦ Write one letter at a time in the middle of the back. Don't attempt to spell the whole word across the back at one time.

♦ Give a clue when a word is over—either by saying aloud, "Next word," or by giving a long pause, or with some other signal such as a light tap on the back to indicate the end of a

MATERIALS NEEDED:
None

AGE OR SKILL LEVEL:
Able to write and spell

word. Two taps can mean "end of sentence," or it can be said aloud.

♦ Alternate who's doing the sending and receiving, unless one child has a strong preference for sending and is paired with another child who has a strong preference for receiving.

INVISIBLE INK MESSAGES

For sending a secret message to a child who's not present in the same room, or even the same city, your kids may want to use invisible ink messages.

Lemon juice makes great invisible ink. After you write with it, it dries to invisibility, but when heated, as by holding it near (not right up against) a light bulb, it darkens and becomes legible again.

A toothpick is a suitable instrument for writing with lemon juice. Lacking that, a small, pointy twig will do. Dip the toothpick in the lemon juice and write your message; as the ink dries it will disappear.

MATERIALS NEEDED:
Paper, lemon juice, toothpick or small twig, heat source such as light bulb

AGE OR SKILL LEVEL:
Able to write and spell

If the messages are being kept in the family, all the participants will know what the secret is to reading the invisible messages: Hold them to a heat source. But if any missives are being sent to others, it's necessary to tell them the secret to making the letters legible. Otherwise the recipient will think some wiseguy has sent a blank piece of paper, and the letter will get no farther than the trash can—or at best will be used to make a paper airplane. (That's one way to get news to travel—but it's not what your kids had in mind!)

WHAT'S THAT?

This guessing game has no winners or losers, but it does offer endless fun for kids. It's an intriguing brain-teaser, one that they'll want to play round after round of.

Two or more can play. Player 1 chooses any item from around the house and, out of range of Player 2's vision, puts it in a large brown paper bag. Player 2 then has to guess what it is. He may have as many guesses as he needs, and no attempt is made to keep track of the number of guesses it takes him to get it right.

Then Player 2 finds something to put in the bag, and Player 1 has to guess what it is. (If there are three kids playing, Player 2 would find something for Player 3 to guess at, and then Player 3 would find something for Player 1 to guess at.)

The object to be guessed at might be a pen, an eggbeater, a sweatsock, a checker, a chess piece, a domino, or even a Christmas ornament. Spectacular incorrect guesses can result in some major hilarity. Players can give up, with no penalty, at any time they feel stumped.

Whether or not your kids will give hints to the identity of the object in the bag, if they are asked, is strictly a matter of house rules.

MATERIALS NEEDED:
Large brown paper bag, various items from around the house

AGE OR SKILL LEVEL:
Four and up

I CAN HELP YOU LEARN

When usually competitive siblings find an activity that induces cooperation, the results can be surprising. I Can Help You Learn is a good example of this type of activity.

When you ask your older child to help her younger sibling to learn a set of facts, memorize a list (state capitals, major bodies of water, key dates in world history), or acquire some other important knowledge, it's certainly possible that she'll resent having this added chore. On the other hand, it's also extremely possible that she'll relish being in the "grown-up" position, or at least a position that puts her clearly superior to the sibling. She's the teacher now, the one possessed of the knowledge, the one teaching this knowledge to the lesser-informed sibling.

Of course, she has to learn those facts first, or at least brush up on them. So if, as is very possible, your older child doesn't know or remember the principal products of the 50 states,

MATERIALS NEEDED:
Whatever books are needed for the information to be acquired

AGE OR SKILL LEVEL:
Six and up and has a younger sibling

or the major world capitals, she's going to be learning (or relearning) them, along with her younger sibling.

If the task is for the older child to teach the names of the first sixteen U.S. Presidents (from Washington to Lincoln) to the younger child, the older one must first learn them herself. She then is to be teacher, prompter, coach, and helper in the younger child's acquisition of that knowledge.

The extent of the information to be learned depends on the capacity of the kids, but don't underestimate your child's potential as a reservoir of knowledge. There are plenty of average seven-year-olds who can rattle off the names of all fifty states.

You needn't wait till the information is assigned in school; it certainly would be a good thing if your son or daughter knew the names of all the provinces of Canada and their capitals *before* any teacher required her to know them. The act of memorization will prepare her for such rote tasks, which will come in handy in school. And the knowledge may come in useful out there in the Real World someday, too. (Suppose one future day your child is a *Jeopardy!* contestant?!)

To ease the kids into memorization tasks, you might want to start them off by getting them to memorize all the cities in which there are teams in the

National Football League, or cities in which Major League Baseball is played. Some other sports/geography statistic may appeal more to them than those do, perhaps a soccer- or hockey- or basketball-related set of statistics.

The kids may surprise you and actually come to value knowledge as a

good thing in and of itself. With the degree of show-off potential that comes with being possessed of knowledge, they may learn to value knowing things as a desirable trait, and even a fun trait.

The kids will also, in the course of this activity, train their minds to absorb and retain information. They will come to understand the ways in which information is organized or categorized. (Example: Sacramento, Indianapolis, and Denver are cities that belong on both the list of state capitals and the list of cities that are home to National Basketball Association teams. Salem, Olympia, and Springfield belong only on the former list, not the latter.)

They'll also be working on a project together happily, harmoniously, and non-competitively.

PRACTICE! PRACTICE!

Virtually any game played for score (or some other means of determining a winner) can also be played for practice. The child who plays basketball can also just shoot hoops for fun—with other kids as well as alone. The child who is into softball or baseball can take batting practice, pitching practice, catching or fielding practice, with no competition, no score, and a lot fewer cries of "He cheated!" (Yes, you might still hear some squabbling over "My turn to bat!" or "Give me the basketball. You had ten

MATERIALS NEEDED:
Varies

AGE OR SKILL LEVEL:
Five and up

shots. It's my turn!" But there'll be a lot less bickering and fighting than in an actual contest.)

Even many board games can be played not-for-score. Take Trivial Pursuit, for instance: You can read the questions aloud and try to come up with the right answers, without moving along the board in an attempt to finish first.

Marbles? Practice shooting. Billiards? Practice shots. Hopscotch? Practice hopping without touching the lines, or practice throwing the potsy into the right square.

Many, many competitive games— or some aspect of them—can be played for practice without actual competition, and when your kids do play competitively again, they'll be better at the game for having practiced.

THE RACE IS ON

Do your kids enjoy novelty races such as sack races, three-legged races, wheelbarrow races, potato races, and other such competitions that involve either an odd form of locomotion (e.g., hopping backward) or the requirement that the runner arrive at the finish line with some other object in a certain condition (e.g., keep your potato on the spoon)?

While *running* such a race would certainly be competitive, *inventing* one isn't, and it can be almost as much fun as actually running it. Tell your

MATERIALS NEEDED:
None, or possibly paper and pen or pencil

AGE OR SKILL LEVEL:
Five and up

kids—or your child and his or her visiting friend—to put their thinking caps on and dream up a new race. They can write down all their ideas if they want, or just keep them in mind till the next time a group of them are looking for something different and competitive to do.

THE JOKE'S ON YOU

Another cooperative venture your kids (or your child and her friends) can engage in is compiling a joke book or riddle book. What kid doesn't love jokes and riddles? What kid doesn't know quite a few? Suppose they wrote down all the jokes they know between them, and then added more jokes they elicited from their friends? They'd have a book—or at least a booklet.

For a *really* ambitious project, they can type the "book" and have it duplicated or type it on your computer, if you have one, and run out multiple copies. But one longhand copy

MATERIALS NEEDED:
Paper and pen or pencil

AGE OR SKILL LEVEL:
Able to write

counts too. Hey, it's their work, their names go on it—and they'll have lots of cooperative fun putting the book together.

If there are any debates as to who gets top billing for authorship, they can draw straws or flip a coin—or adhere to the old solution of alphabetical order.

HOUSE OF CARDS

We've all tried to build a house of cards at one time or another, with greater or lesser success. Your kids can work on such a project together—and with four hands working on the construction, a taller tower is likely to result. Two hands can hold a card in place while another two hands place the next pair of cards on it, or one child can hold two cards upright while another child places the cross-piece that will hold them in place.

There's real cooperation—with visible results.

MATERIALS NEEDED:
Deck of cards
(an incomplete deck
is fine)

AGE OR SKILL LEVEL:
Seven and up

HOW MANY REAL FEET?

How many feet is the length of your hallway? No, not how many times twelve inches—how many *real* feet? Kid feet. Not the twelve-inch, ruler kind of feet, but *real life* feet. Your kids probably don't even know how many ruler-feet the various rooms of your house measure—and they probably don't care. Measuring feet are abstract. They aren't anything most kids can relate to.

Ah, but *real* feet. … How many times can your kids put heel to toe and walk a straight line down the length of your hallway from one end to the other? How many times will they put heel to toe if they walk around the yard as close to the house as they can get? What's the difference between that number and the number of steps they take if they walk around the edge of the yard, as *far away from* the house as they can get?

There are lots of measurements your kids can take with their feet and/or their hands, from room lengths and widths to door heights and bed lengths. Just how many rooms and items they're willing to measure will depend on whether they're math nuts or not. If your child has "engi-neer" written all over his future, he may not be willing to stop measuring when you call dinner; the average child will measure the length and width of a few rooms, maybe a couple of pieces of furniture, and call it quits.

> **MATERIALS NEEDED:**
> None, or possibly pen or pencil and paper
>
> **AGE OR SKILL LEVEL:**
> Able to count to perhaps thirty

Though this is a diversion that doesn't *require* more than one participant, two or more kids can easily get involved through having one child measure the length of a room while the other measures the width, or having one child measure one room while the other measures another, after which they can compare their findings. Or one can measure the number of real-life feet across a room while the other measures hands. Or have one child take the conventional measurements of a room and have the other child measure how many real-life feet wide and long it measures by comparison.

"FOUR OUT OF FIVE KIDS SURVEYED SAID..."

Although this activity, like a couple of others in the book, will especially appeal to kids destined to grow up as statisticians, it will also be fun for lots of other kids as well. No math is needed here, no love of numbers. As Sgt. Friday would have said, "Just the facts."

And what *are* the facts? That's what your little survey-takers are going to find out. What are the questions? That's for them to decide. What would they like to know?

The most popular (or most unusual) pets? Pet names? Typical dinnertimes in households in your area? Favorite TV shows? Favorite entertainers? Favorite books? Favorite songs? Favorite cereals? Favorite dinners? Favorite ice cream flavors? Favorite TV characters? How many kids have

MATERIALS NEEDED:
Paper and pen or pencil

AGE OR SKILL LEVEL:
Six and up

grandparents living nearby? What states have kids visited? What other cities have kids lived in? What countries do kids' families come from? How many kids have ever been to Disney World? How many kids have ever gotten 100 on a math test? How many kids have ever...?

They can take a survey at school, call friends on the phone, ask around the playground or park, or even ring doorbells of kids they know. Of course it won't be a scientific sampling, but it will be interesting. And if they ask such questions as, "What's your bedtime?" or "What chores are you expected to do around the house?" or "What's your allowance?" they might find out you're not treating them so unfairly after all!

214